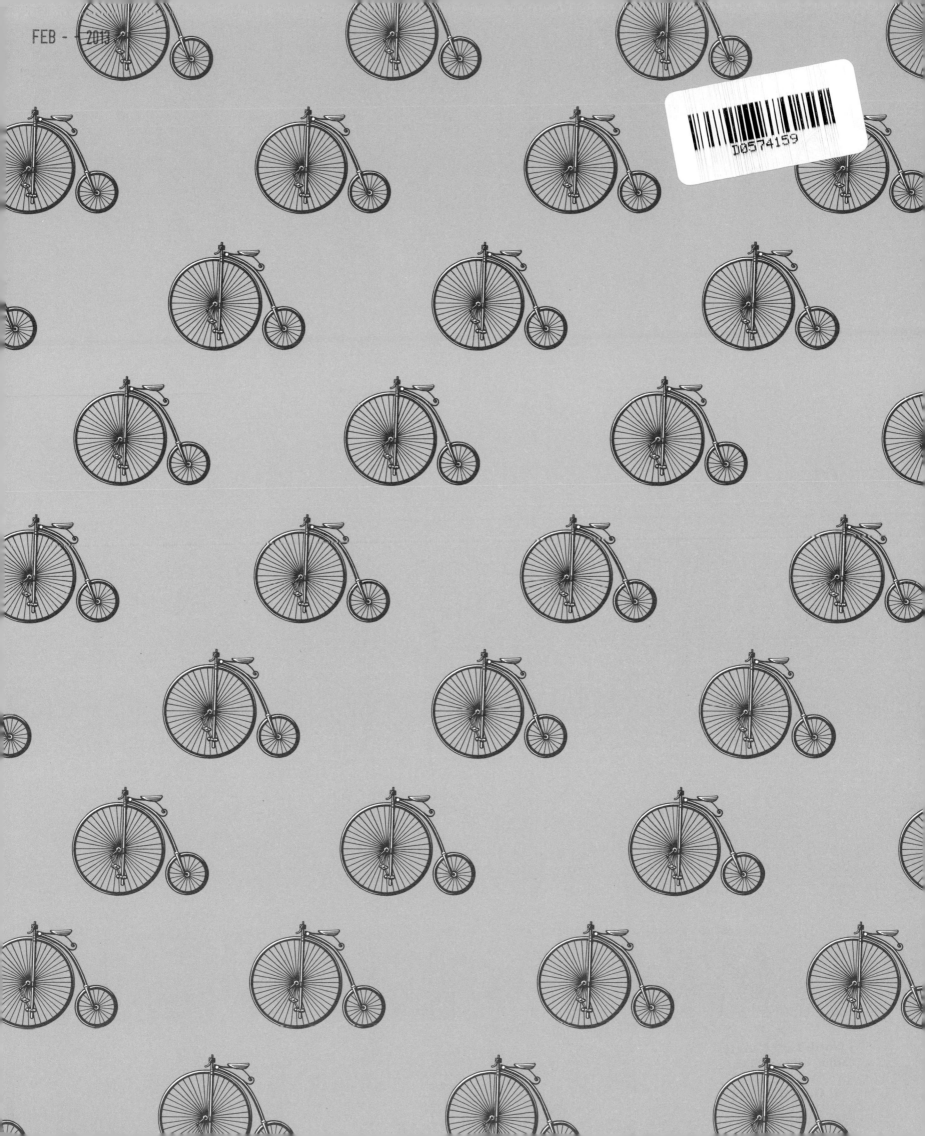

Great Inventions

The Nature Company Discoveries Library published by Time-Life Books

Conceived and produced by
Weldon Owen Pty Limited
43 Victoria Street, McMahons Point,
NSW, 2060, Australia
A member of the
Weldon Owen Group of Companies
Sydney • San Francisco • London
Copyright 1995 © US Weldon Owen Reference Inc.
Copyright 1995 © Weldon Owen Pty Ltd

THE NATURE COMPANY
Priscilla Wrubel, Ed Strobin, Steve Manning,
Georganne Papac, Tracy Fortini

TIME LIFE BOOKS
Time-Life Books is a division of Time Life Inc.,
a wholly owned subsidiary of THE TIME INC.
BOOK COMPANY

Vice President and Publisher: Terry Newell
Editorial Director: Donia A. Steele
Director of New Product Development:
Regina Hall
Director of Sales: Neil Levin
Director of Custom Publishing:
Frances C. Mangan
Director of Financial Operations: J. Brian Birky

WELDON OWEN Pty Ltd
Chairman: Kevin Weldon
President: John Owen
Publisher: Sheena Coupe
Managing Editor: Rosemary McDonald
Project Editor: Helen Bateman
Text Editors: Claire Craig, Tracy Tucker
Editorial Assistant: Selena Quintrell Hand
Educational Consultants: Richard L. Needham,
Deborah A. Powell
Art Director: Sue Burk
Designers: Juliet Cohen, Kylie Mulquin
Assistant Designers: Gary Fletcher, Robyn Latimer,
Angela Pelizzari
Visual Research Coordinator: Jenny Mills

Visual Research: Karen Burgess, Carel Fillmer,
Kathy Gerrard, Fran Meagher, Kristina Sturm
Production Director: Mick Bagnato
Production Manager: Simone Perryman
Vice-President, International Sales:
Stuart Laurence
Coeditions Director: Derek Barton

Text: Richard Wood

Illustrators: Graham Back; David Boehm;
Gregory Bridges; Leslye Cole; Christer Eriksson;
Mike Golding; Christa Hook/Bernard Thornton
Artists, UK; Richard Hook/Bernard Thornton
Artists, UK; Gillian Jenkins; Mike Lamble;
Connell Lee; Iain McKellar; David Nelson;
Stephen Seymour/Bernard Thornton Artists, UK;
Ray Sim; Mark Sofilas; Kevin Stead;
Ross Watton/Garden Studio; Rod Westblade

Library of Congress
Cataloging-in-Publication Data
Great inventions / consulting editor,
    Richard Wood.

        p. cm -- (Discoveries Library)

    Includes index.
    ISBN 0-7835-4766-8

    1. Inventions--History--Juvenile literature.
[1.Inventions.] I. Title. II. Series: Discoveries
Library (Alexandria, Va.)

T15.W797 1995

609--dc20   95-12947

Manufactured by Mandarin Offset
Printed in China

A Weldon Owen Production

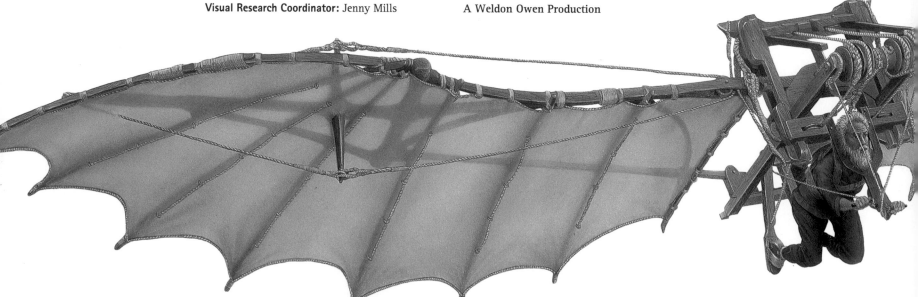

THE NATURE COMPANY
DISCOVERIES
LIBRARY

Great Inventions

CONSULTING EDITOR

Richard Wood
Curator, Engineering and Design,
Museum of Applied Arts and Sciences, Sydney

TIME
LIFE
BOOKS

Contents

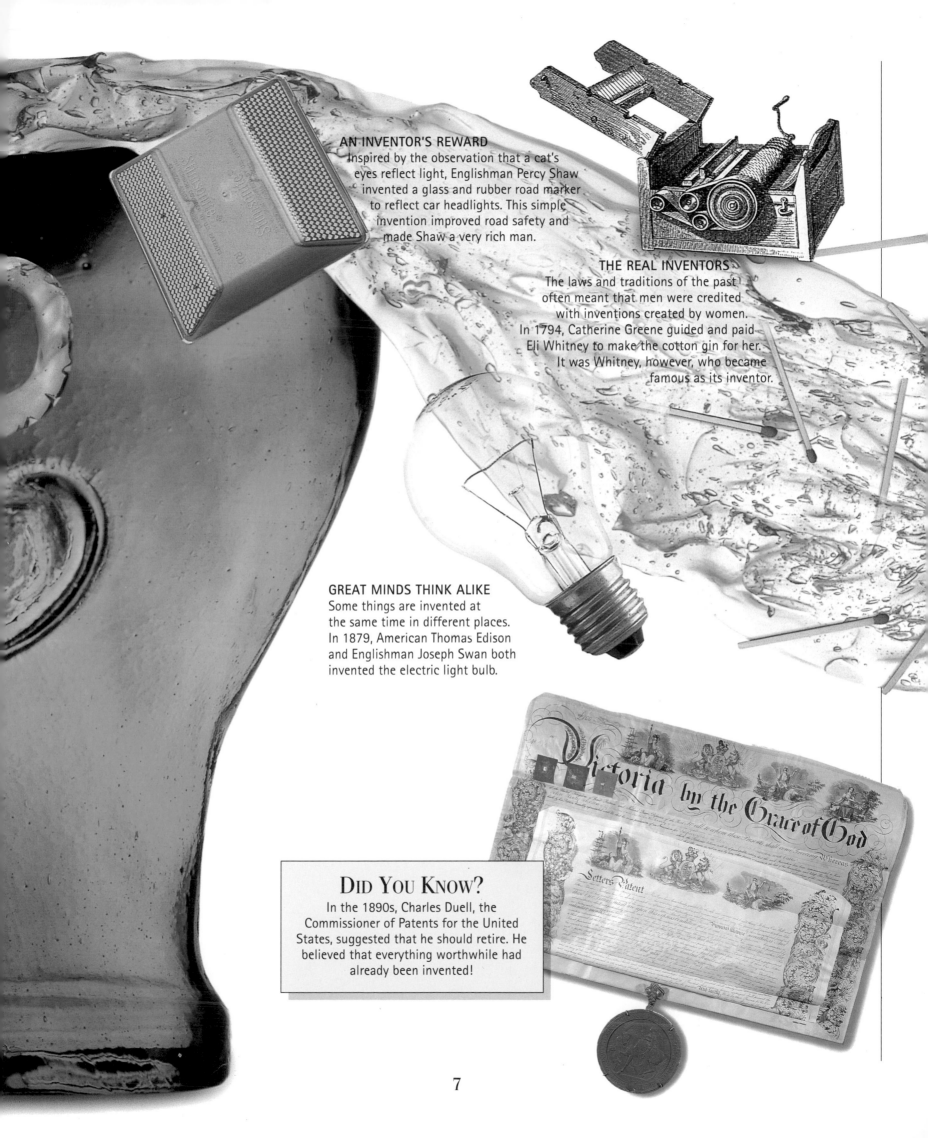

AN INVENTOR'S REWARD

Inspired by the observation that a cat's eyes reflect light, Englishman Percy Shaw invented a glass and rubber road marker to reflect car headlights. This simple invention improved road safety and made Shaw a very rich man.

THE REAL INVENTORS

The laws and traditions of the past often meant that men were credited with inventions created by women. In 1794, Catherine Greene guided and paid Eli Whitney to make the cotton gin for her. It was Whitney, however, who became famous as its inventor.

GREAT MINDS THINK ALIKE

Some things are invented at the same time in different places. In 1879, American Thomas Edison and Englishman Joseph Swan both invented the electric light bulb.

DID YOU KNOW?

In the 1890s, Charles Duell, the Commissioner of Patents for the United States, suggested that he should retire. He believed that everything worthwhile had already been invented!

LIGHT UP

Gustave Pasch of Sweden patented safety matches in 1845, but they were not manufactured until 1855. Earlier types ignited without warning, or gave off dangerous gases.

A QUICK SHAVE

In 1901, a traveling salesman named King Camp Gillette invented the disposable razor blade in the United States.

AN EXPENSIVE WASH

Soap was invented in Sumeria 4,000 years ago, but it was not until the 1820s that it became cheap enough for most people to buy.

SAFETY PIN

In 1849, Englishman Charles Rowley and American Walter Hunt both invented a clever device—the safety pin.

BUTTON UP

Buttons have been used since ancient times. The modern two-holed button is thought to have been invented in Scotland about 4,000 years ago.

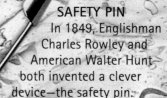

• EVERYDAY LIFE •

Simple Things

We use buttons, bottles, knives, nails, safety pins, combs, coat hangers and other simple inventions every day. What would we do without them? Imagine a supermarket without canned foods, bread, ice cream, cartons of milk or packets of crackers! People are constantly re-inventing simple things, such as toothbrushes and bottle caps, by using new ideas, materials and technologies. Other inventions, such as pins and coat hangers, were perfect when they were invented and have changed very little since. A special word for simple, yet ingenious, inventions was coined in New York in 1886. Frenchman Monsieur Gaget sold thousands of miniature models of the Statue of Liberty to American sightseers. The New Yorkers who bought these statues called them "gadgets," and the word has been used ever since to describe clever but simple devices.

LOCK AND KEY

In 2000 BC, the Egyptians made wooden locks and keys to secure royal treasures. These locks and keys were decorated with gold to show their importance. In 1865, Linus Yale Jr. patented a drum-and-pin lock that could be mass-produced.

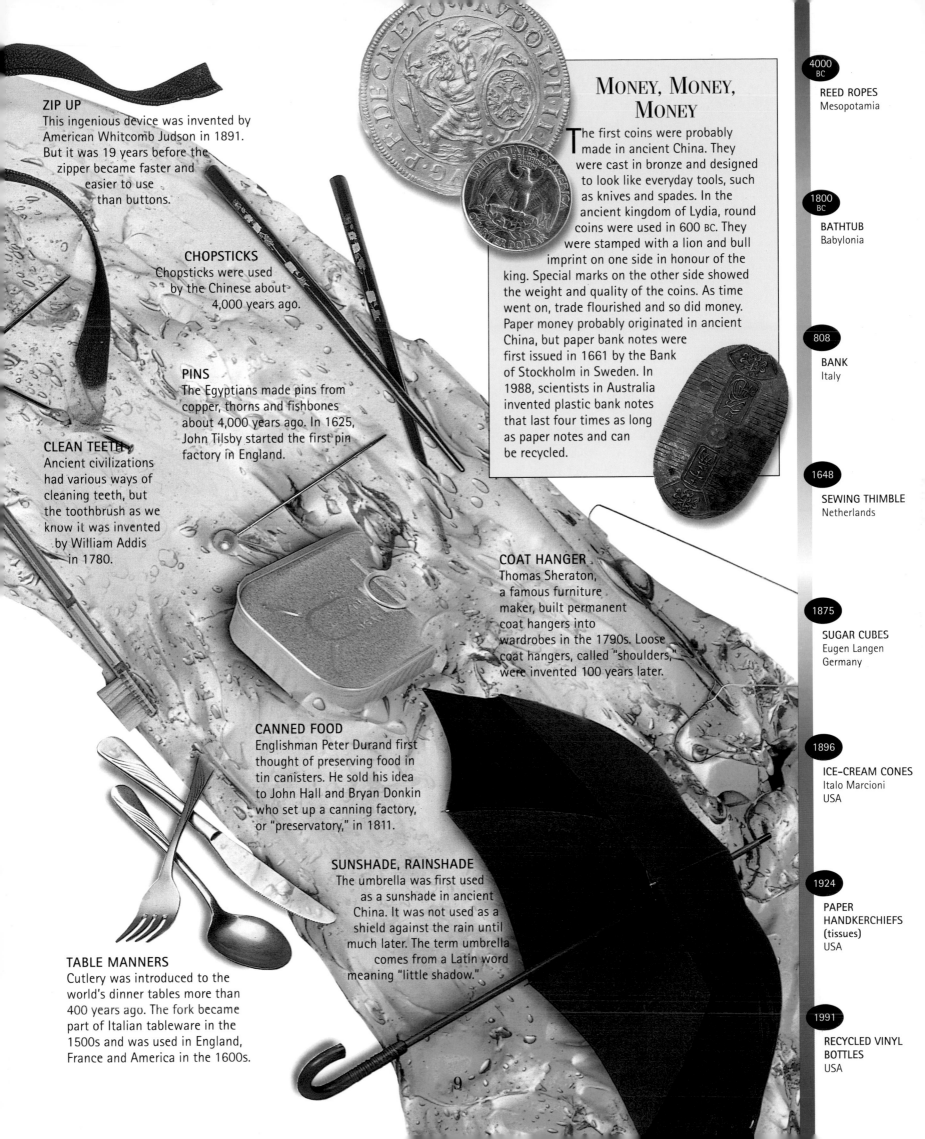

ZIP UP
This ingenious device was invented by American Whitcomb Judson in 1891. But it was 19 years before the zipper became faster and easier to use than buttons.

CHOPSTICKS
Chopsticks were used by the Chinese about 4,000 years ago.

PINS
The Egyptians made pins from copper, thorns and fishbones about 4,000 years ago. In 1625, John Tilsby started the first pin factory in England.

CLEAN TEETH
Ancient civilizations had various ways of cleaning teeth, but the toothbrush as we know it was invented by William Addis in 1780.

TABLE MANNERS
Cutlery was introduced to the world's dinner tables more than 400 years ago. The fork became part of Italian tableware in the 1500s and was used in England, France and America in the 1600s.

CANNED FOOD
Englishman Peter Durand first thought of preserving food in tin canisters. He sold his idea to John Hall and Bryan Donkin who set up a canning factory, or "preservatory," in 1811.

COAT HANGER
Thomas Sheraton, a famous furniture maker, built permanent coat hangers into wardrobes in the 1790s. Loose coat hangers, called "shoulders," were invented 100 years later.

SUNSHADE, RAINSHADE
The umbrella was first used as a sunshade in ancient China. It was not used as a shield against the rain until much later. The term umbrella comes from a Latin word meaning "little shadow."

MONEY, MONEY, MONEY

The first coins were probably made in ancient China. They were cast in bronze and designed to look like everyday tools, such as knives and spades. In the ancient kingdom of Lydia, round coins were used in 600 BC. They were stamped with a lion and bull imprint on one side in honour of the king. Special marks on the other side showed the weight and quality of the coins. As time went on, trade flourished and so did money. Paper money probably originated in ancient China, but paper bank notes were first issued in 1661 by the Bank of Stockholm in Sweden. In 1988, scientists in Australia invented plastic bank notes that last four times as long as paper notes and can be recycled.

4000 BC
REED ROPES
Mesopotamia

1800 BC
BATHTUB
Babylonia

808
BANK
Italy

1648
SEWING THIMBLE
Netherlands

1875
SUGAR CUBES
Eugen Langen
Germany

1896
ICE-CREAM CONES
Italo Marcioni
USA

1924
PAPER HANDKERCHIEFS
(tissues)
USA

1991
RECYCLED VINYL BOTTLES
USA

THE LOOKING GLASS
Glass mirrors were invented in Venice, Italy, perhaps 600 years ago. They were made by sticking a very thin layer of tinfoil onto glass using mercury.

A royal treat
Ice cream was probably first enjoyed in ancient China. It was re-invented in Europe in the 1300s and became a popular dessert among royalty.

• EVERYDAY LIFE •

Around the House

We use household inventions so frequently, it seems as if we have always had them. But these everyday items and devices were once new and exciting. Inventions for the house were designed to take the effort out of household chores. Before the vacuum cleaner, people would laboriously beat their carpets to remove the dust; before the lawn mower, cutting grass was a back-breaking task done by hand with a scythe. Before the electric refrigerator, food needed to be bought daily and any leftovers thrown away. When they were first produced, most household inventions were handmade, unreliable and expensive. Mass production made many goods cheaper, more reliable and available to everyone. Household inventions are constantly being improved and updated. What labor-saving inventions will we use in houses of the future?

FRIDGES FOR THE FUTURE
The first electric refrigerators were cooled by poisonous substances, such as ammonia. After the 1930s, manufacturers used a non-toxic substance called Freon. But Freon was found to cause the breakdown of ozone in the Earth's atmosphere. This environmentally friendly fridge was invented in Germany in 1991.

10

Frozen food
After observing how the Inuit (Eskimos) preserved their fish, Clarence Birdseye saw the potential for quick-freezing many foods. Birdseye introduced frozen foods to American stores in about 1930.

Margarine
A shortage of butter in France in the 1860s led Emperor Napoleon III to encourage the development of a substitute. In 1869, Hippolyte Mège-Mouriès invented a paste made from animal fats. He called it margarine.

"It Beats as it Sweeps as it Cleans"

In 1901, Hubert Cecil Booth was convinced he could build a machine that picked up and filtered dust using suction. He did just that, but the cleaner was so large it had to be set on a trolley and needed two people to operate it. James Murray Spangler invented a more portable model and in 1908 patented the Electrical Vacuum Carpet Sweeper. Spangler sold his idea to a man named William Hoover. His surname and the above slogan became household words in many countries.

Chocolate
Chocolate is made from the seeds of a tropical tree called *cacao*. Early Central and South Americans crushed the seeds to make a drink. The first chocolate bar was made in Switzerland in 1819 by François-Louis Cailler.

SEWING MACHINE
In the early 1800s, the first sewing machines were not welcomed by tailors, who thought their jobs were under threat. In 1851, Isaac Singer invented the first efficient domestic sewing machine.

DID YOU KNOW?
During the Second World War, two scientists developed a device to produce microwaves. Little did they know their work to improve radar would later be used to develop a new cooking appliance—the microwave oven.

RESTROOM
The flush toilet was invented by Sir John Harington in 1589. He installed one in his own house and one in the house of his godmother, Queen Elizabeth I of England. But they did not become common until nearly 200 years later.

Perfect packaging
Convenient "waxed cardboard" cartons with pull-out spouts were invented in Sweden by Ruben Rausing in 1951.

100 BC
SAUNA BATH
Finland

1795
CORKSCREW
Samuel Hershaw
England

1857
TOILET PAPER
USA

1886
DISHWASHER
Josephine Cochrane
USA

1901
ELECTRIC WASHING MACHINE
Alva Fisher
USA

1909
ELECTRIC TOASTER
USA

1917
ELECTRIC HAND DRILL
Duncan Black and Alonso Decker
USA

1926
AEROSOL SPRAY
Erik Rotheim
Norway

1945
MICROWAVE OVEN
Percy Le Baron Spencer
USA

1985
SOAPLESS ULTRASONIC WASHER
Nihon University
Japan

At a Factory

Long ago, members of a family or tribe would make everything they needed by hand. As the population grew, people worked together in factories. In 1798, American Eli Whitney invented mass production. He received an order for 10,000 guns, but realized it was impossible for craftspeople to produce this quantity in the time available. He decided to divide the work up into separate jobs, so that different people could make different parts of the gun, which was then put together later. At the same time in England, James Watt's new steam engines were installed in factories, and soon the Industrial Revolution began. The new steam factories employed many people, but the work was dangerous, cramped, time-consuming and often boring. Many factories today offer good lighting, filtered air, protective clothing and rest breaks. Robots are used for the worst jobs, and people work fewer hours in safer conditions.

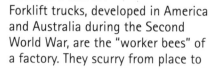

FORKLIFT TRUCK
Forklift trucks, developed in America and Australia during the Second World War, are the "worker bees" of a factory. They scurry from place to place carrying heavy loads on wood or plastic pallets.

PROTECTIVE CLOTHING
The heat, the cold and dangerous chemicals used in today's factories mean that suits such as this are needed to protect the worker from danger.

KEEPING IT ALL TOGETHER
Handmade metal nails were first used by the Egyptians to hold coffins together 5,000 years ago. Tiny metal screws for joining wood date back to 1760. Before welding, metals were joined with pins or rivets.

WORK TIME

The time clock was invented by American W. H. Bundy in 1885. Workers were given their own specially numbered key, which they inserted into the clock when they arrived at work. This key activated the clock to print their key number and their arrival time on a strip of paper. When the workers were ready to leave, they repeated this process, so their employer could check the number of hours they had worked. The Australian phrases to "bundy on," meaning to arrive at work, and to "bundy off," meaning to leave work, have helped to keep the inventor's name alive.

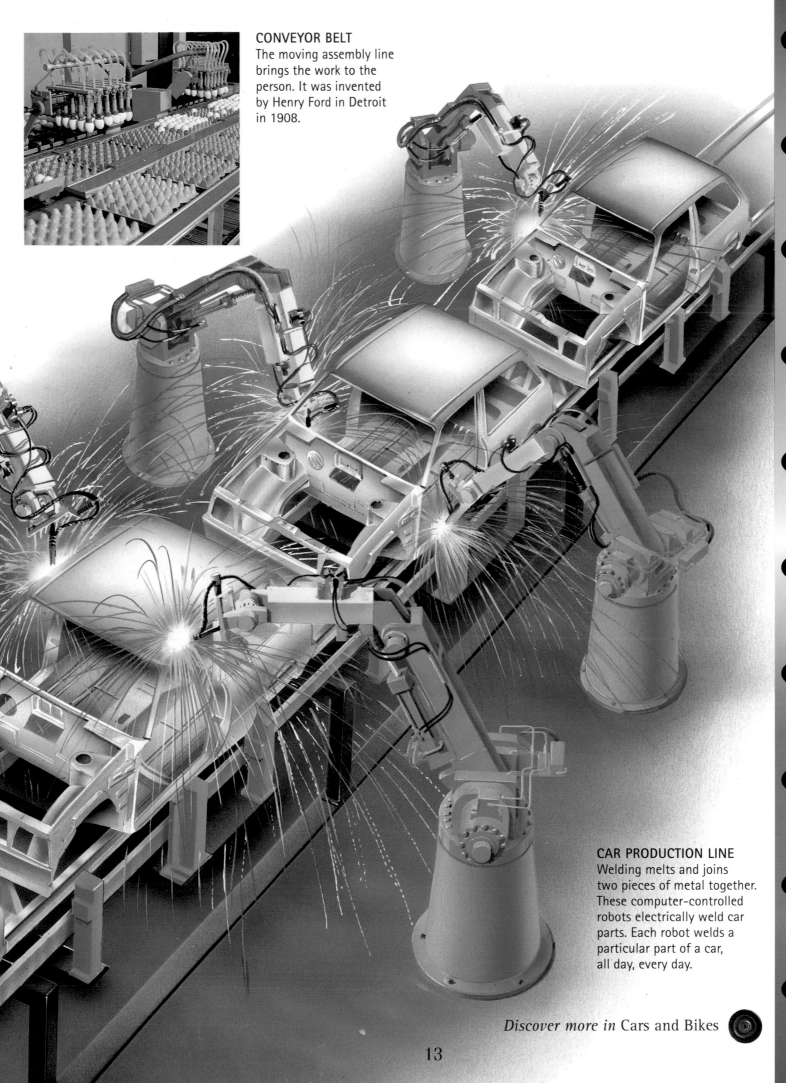

CONVEYOR BELT
The moving assembly line brings the work to the person. It was invented by Henry Ford in Detroit in 1908.

CAR PRODUCTION LINE
Welding melts and joins two pieces of metal together. These computer-controlled robots electrically weld car parts. Each robot welds a particular part of a car, all day, every day.

Discover more in Cars and Bikes

1500 BC
IRON SMELTING
Asia Minor

430 BC
PULLEY WHEEL
Archytas of Tarentum
Greece

287 BC
CRANE
Archimedes
Greece

200 BC
CRANK HANDLE
China

1550
NUTS, BOLTS AND WRENCHES
France

1804
PATTERN-WEAVING LOOM
Joseph-Marie Jacquard
France

1856
STEEL MAKING
Henry Bessemer
England

1903
OXYACETYLENE WELDING TORCH
Fouch and Picard
France

1946
ROBOT AUTOMATION
Delmar Harder
USA

1983
ROBOT-MAKING ROBOT
Japan

On a Farm

The plow and irrigation have tamed more farmland than any other farming inventions. People first grew crops in the Middle East about 10,000 years ago, but planting, harvesting and watering them by hand was a slow process. In Egypt and India, nearly 4,500 years later, farmers prepared the ground for planting with wooden plows pulled by oxen. The Egyptians invented a machine called a shaduf, which helped them take water from the River Nile to irrigate or water their crops. Barbed wire was another great farming invention. Farmers used it to divide huge areas of Africa, North America and Australia into separate wheat, cattle and sheep farms in the 1800s. These enormous new farms revolutionized farming. Farmers now needed faster ways of harvesting grain, wool, meat and milk. The old methods were soon replaced by machines that did the work of hundreds of people.

FORK
Iron forks were invented by the Romans. "Pitchforks" were used to "pitch" or stack hay in the field.

RAKE
Wooden rakes were invented in Europe in about AD 500 to gather grain that had been threshed or beaten off its stalks.

SPADE
Wooden spades with iron blades were invented by the Romans about 2,000 years ago.

BARBED WIRE
In 1867, American Lucien Smith invented barbed wire and made it possible for farmers to fence off their lands.

FOUR JOBS IN ONE
In 1884, Australian Hugh McKay invented the horse-drawn harvester. It combined cutting, threshing, winnowing and bagging wheat grain into one operation. Combine harvesters with gasoline or diesel engines are now used 24 hours a day, with lights at night, to harvest the crops.

WATERING THE CROPS
The Egyptian shaduf is a little like a seesaw. A long wooden pole, balanced on a crossbeam, has a rope and bucket at one end, and a heavy stone weight to counterbalance it at the other. The weight of the rock makes it easier to lift a heavy bucket of water.

PLOW
Plows made from wood and stag antlers were invented in Egypt and India about 5,500 years ago. Simple ox-drawn plows are still used on family farms in many countries.

DID YOU KNOW?
Superphosphates—artificial chemicals that enrich the soil—were invented by Sir John Bennett Lawes in England in 1842. But fertilizers often run into the rivers and oceans, killing fish and making algae grow.

TRACTOR
Three-wheeled steam tractors, built by the Case company of America in 1829, were very heavy and often became stuck in the soft soil. Modern tractors were pioneered by Henry Ford in 1907.

15

1794
COTTON GIN (SEPARATOR)
Catherine Greene and Eli Whitney
USA

1831
GRAIN REAPER (CUTTER)
Cyrus McCormick
USA

1833
STEEL PLOW
John Lane
USA

1860
HYDROPONICS
Ferdinand Gustav Sachs and Knopp
Germany

1868
GRANNY SMITH APPLE
Maria Smith
Australia

1889
MODERN MILKING MACHINE
William Murchland
Scotland

1924
AERIAL CROP DUSTING
USA

1939
DDT PESTICIDE
Muller and Weissmann
Switzerland

1975
AXIAL COMBINE HARVESTER
International Harvester
New Holland, USA

At School and the Office

D uring some stage of their lives, people in many countries spend time in schools and offices. Schools were first set up in Greece between 800 BC and 400 BC to teach boys subjects such as mathematics and astronomy. In the 1800s, people were employed in offices to monitor the staff and accounts of the first factories. Today, on a desk at school or the office you will find inventions large and small. It is hard to imagine our lives without them. Desks would be strewn with papers because we would not have paperclips or staplers to keep them together. How would you write without pens and pencils and make straight lines without rulers? How would you cut paper without scissors? In fact, if the Chinese had not invented paper, there would be nothing to write on, cut or keep in an orderly pile.

BLACKBOARD
James Pillans, a Scottish teacher, invented the blackboard in 1814 so that all his students would be able to see the maps he drew.

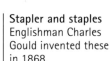

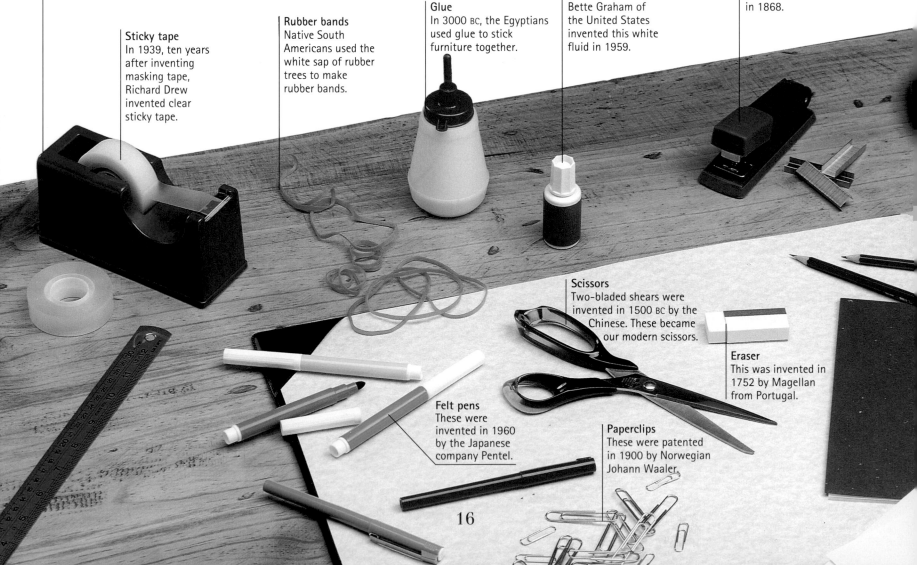

Sticky tape
In 1939, ten years after inventing masking tape, Richard Drew invented clear sticky tape.

Rubber bands
Native South Americans used the white sap of rubber trees to make rubber bands.

Glue
In 3000 BC, the Egyptians used glue to stick furniture together.

Correction fluid
Bette Graham of the United States invented this white fluid in 1959.

Stapler and staples
Englishman Charles Gould invented these in 1868.

Scissors
Two-bladed shears were invented in 1500 BC by the Chinese. These became our modern scissors.

Eraser
This was invented in 1752 by Magellan from Portugal.

Felt pens
These were invented in 1960 by the Japanese company Pentel.

Paperclips
These were patented in 1900 by Norwegian Johann Waaler.

16

DID YOU KNOW?

Inventions are often simple but ingenious solutions to problems. Arthur Fry kept losing his place in a hymn book. He put some weak glue on his page markers so they could be stuck on one page, then moved to another. Sticky notes were invented.

HITTING THE KEYS

Carlos Gliddens and Christopher Sholes named their typewriter the "literary piano". In 1873, the Remington Fire Arms Company undertook to manufacture it, and in 1876, it was displayed at the Centennial Exposition in the United States.

MOVING LIGHT

The desk lamp is a little like an arm. It can be moved about for close work or kept in the same position. An adjustable desk lamp was designed by George Carwardine in 1934.

Pencils
Soft graphite was used for pencils in England from 1564.

PHOTOCOPIER

The first photocopiers used messy chemicals and sensitive papers to photograph documents. In 1938, Chester Carlson invented a dry copying process that used plain paper. The first photocopiers of this kind were sold in 1959.

Sticky notes
These were invented in 1980 by American Arthur Fry.

FAX MACHINE

Around 1900, German scientist Arthur Korn invented an electric cell that could detect dark and light areas on paper. He used it to send a photograph by telephone line from Germany to England in 1907. Almost 70 years passed before people realized how useful this invention would be in the office. The fax (which is short for facsimile, meaning an exact copy or a reproduction) now plays an important part in offices. This machine makes it possible to communicate instantly with people all over the world.

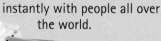

Discover more in From Quill to Press

17

400 BC
SCHOOL
Greece

1806
CARBON-COPY PAPER
R. Wedgewood
England

1837
SHORTHAND WRITING
Isaac Pitman
England

1858
PENCIL WITH ERASER ATTACHED
Hyman Lipman
USA

1901
ELECTRIC TYPEWRITER
Thaddeus Cahill
USA

1903
WET PHOTOCOPIER
G. C. Beidler
USA

1959
CORRECTION FLUID
Bette Graham
USA

1990
NO-LICK STAMPS
Australia Post
Australia

At Play

People are always inventing ways to have fun. The Egyptians threw stone balls at upright pins in a game similar to bowling about 5,000 years ago. The Greeks played "soccer" with inflated animal bladders about 2,500 years ago. Some games seem timeless—hopscotch, marbles, tick-tack-toe and rope skipping are as popular today as when they were first played. Dolls have delighted young and old for centuries. They have been made of many different materials, from apples and animal skins to china and plastic. In 1823, baby dolls were made to cry. Soon, they were talking as well. Today, the games industry is booming as inventors create new and exciting games that challenge all who play them.

CHECKMATE
Chess was invented in about AD 500 in India. The moves we play today were first used in Europe in the mid-1500s. The winning position "checkmate" comes from *shah mat*, Arabic for "the king is dead."

BARBIE DOLL
In 1958, Ruth Handler invented Barbie, a dress-up doll complete with a wardrobe of clothes and a way of life. More than one billion Barbie dolls have been sold in 140 countries.

NINE OR TEN PINS?
In 1845, nine-pin bowling had become so popular in the state of Connecticut that it encouraged heavy gambling. A law was passed that banned the game of "bowling at nine pins." The eager bowlers added a tenth pin and kept on bowling!

DID YOU KNOW?

The very first roller skates, invented by a Belgian musician Joseph Merlin in 1760, had wheels in one line—similar to today's rollerblades.

LEGO™

The Danish word *leg-godt* means to play well. Ole Kirk Christiansen chose the name "Lego" for his line of toys. By 1955, his toy plastic bricks that can be joined to construct things such as buildings, machines, people and animals were known as Lego all over the world.

GAMES, GAMES, GAMES

In 1972, American Nolan Bushnell invented the first successful computer game. It was like table tennis, and was called *Pong*. In 1978, *Space Invaders* was introduced and became a big success. Today's electronic games, such as *Where in the World is Carmen Sandiego?*, use full color animation, speed and constantly changing tactics to outwit even the best human players. The computer game *Lunicus* (below) pits players against a giant bee in the year 2000.

2450 BC
DOMINOES
Mesopotamia

1200 BC
CHECKERS
Egypt, Sri Lanka

1450
GOLF
Scotland

1823
CRYING DOLLS
Johann Maelzel
Belgium

1850
MAH–JONG
China

1882
JUDO
Jigoro Kano
Japan

1891
BASKETBALL
James Naismith
USA

1929
YO–YO
Donald Dwean
USA

1931
MONOPOLY
Charles Darrow
USA

1992
VIDEO BOARD GAME
Brett Clements and Phillip Tanner
Australia

People Movers

A SMALL BEGINNING
Walter Hancock's steam-powered motor bus of 1831 (known as the *infant*) could carry only ten passengers. Buses today, such as this English double-decker, have gasoline or diesel engines, and can carry more than 70 people.

Mass transportation was invented to carry large numbers of people at one time. The first omnibus (a Latin word that means "for everyone") was built by Englishman George Shillibeer in 1829. It had 22 seats and was pulled by three horses. Robert Stephenson's steam locomotive, the *Rocket*, traveled so fast in 1829 that Dr Dionysys Lardner was moved to predict: "passengers, unable to breathe, will suffocate". People loved train travel, and railway tracks spread across the countryside like giant spider webs. In 1863, railways went underground in London, and five years later they were built overhead in New York. Streetcars soon appeared in city streets everywhere, and in huge stores people rode on escalators invented by Jesse Reno in 1894 as rides in a New York amusement park.

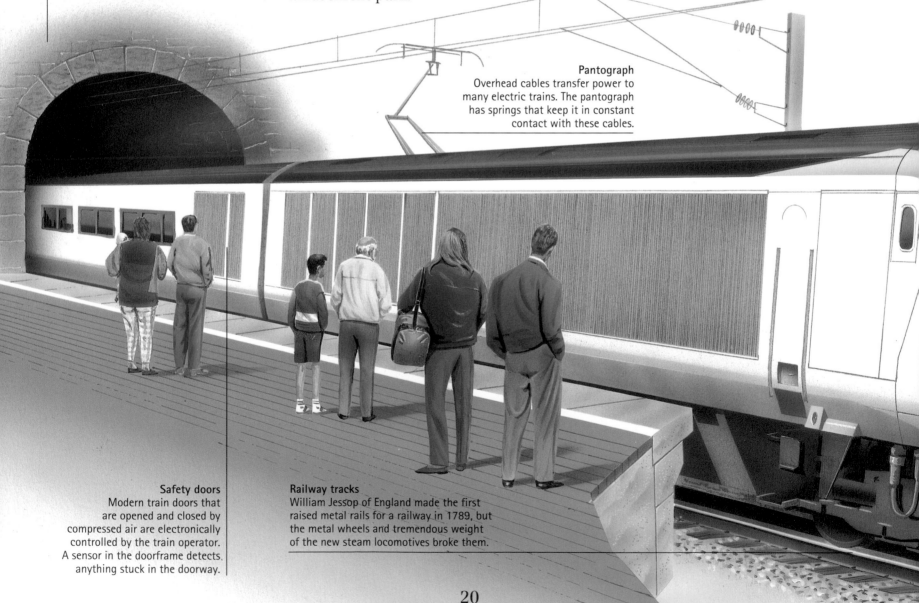

Pantograph
Overhead cables transfer power to many electric trains. The pantograph has springs that keep it in constant contact with these cables.

Safety doors
Modern train doors that are opened and closed by compressed air are electronically controlled by the train operator. A sensor in the doorframe detects anything stuck in the doorway.

Railway tracks
William Jessop of England made the first raised metal rails for a railway in 1789, but the metal wheels and tremendous weight of the new steam locomotives broke them.

20

AROUND THE WHEEL

The invention of the wheel made an enormous difference to people in many countries. The first wheels are thought to have been developed in about 3500 BC in southwest Asia. They were made from planks of wood cut into a circle. These solid, heavy wheels were replaced eventually by lighter spoked wheels, a design which was perfected by Leonardo da Vinci in the 1400s. Wheels with wire spokes were developed in about 1800, and in 1895 André and Edouard Michelin introduced air-filled tires on cars.

CABLE TRAM

Cable trams such as this one have been running up and down the steep hills of San Francisco, California since 1873. They are pulled along by a cable that is set inside a groove in the road.

ON TRACK

Monorails glide along a single track above crowded streets. They look very modern, but a cable-powered monorail took passengers around the Lyon Exposition in France as early as 1872.

ELECTRIC TRAIN

This is one of the Eurostar trains, a fleet of electric trains in Europe. The French TGV—one of the fastest electric trains—travels at an average speed of 161 miles (260 km) per hour between Paris and Lyon.

DID YOU KNOW?

The first electric traffic light was invented in 1914 by Alfred Benesch of Cleveland, Ohio. It consisted of only one light: red—the signal to stop. The yellow and green traffic lights were added in New York in 1918.

1640
TAXI FLEET
Nicholas Sauvage
France

1802
STEAM LOCOMOTIVE
Richard Trevithick
Wales

1857
STEAM SAFETY ELEVATOR
Elisha Otis
USA

1879
ELECTRIC LOCOMOTIVE
Werner von Siemens and Johann Malske
Germany

1888
ELECTRIC TRAMWAY
Frank J. Sprague
USA

1908
CABLE CAR
Switzerland

1964
VERY FAST TRAIN
Japanese National Railways
Japan

1981
SUPER FAST TRAIN (TGV)
France

Cars and Bikes

Cars and bikes revolutionized transportation for people everywhere. Bikes gave everyone the freedom to travel where they wished, over long distances and at speeds of up to 43 miles (70 km) per hour—downhill, anyway. The design of bikes changed considerably, from the dandy horse to the penny-farthing, before the modern bike was invented in 1879. The first motor car was a three-wheeled road steamer, invented by Nicolas-Joseph Cugnot in 1769. It traveled at 3 miles (5 km) per hour and could be overtaken by most people walking at a brisk pace! Handmade, gasoline-engined cars were invented in 1885 by German Carl Benz, but they were very expensive. When cars such as the Volkswagen Beetle were mass-produced in the 1940s, they became more affordable. Millions of people could now enjoy the pleasures of driving—and the horrors of traffic jams.

A CLASSIC HARLEY
In Germany in 1894, brothers Heinrich and Wilhelm Hildebrand and Alois Wolfmüller built the first motorbikes to have two-stroke engines and pneumatic tires. This motorbike is a 1917 model Harley Davidson.

DID YOU KNOW?

In 1970, Gary Gabelich traveled faster by car than anyone else ever has. In the "Blue Flame," he sped along the Bonneville Salt Flats in Utah at 628.9 miles (1,014.3 km) per hour.

Dandy horse
1790

Penny-farthing
1870

Safety bike
1879

Aerodynamic bike
Early 1980s

A POPULAR BEETLE
Commonly known as the Beetle, this Volkswagen (VW) is one of the most popular cars in the world. About 23 million have been produced since the first model hit the road in 1936.

Back-to-front car
The VW has a most unusual design element: the engine is at the back and the spare tire is at the front.

Headlights
Driving at night was very difficult until 1925, when headlamps that had both short and long beams of light were invented.

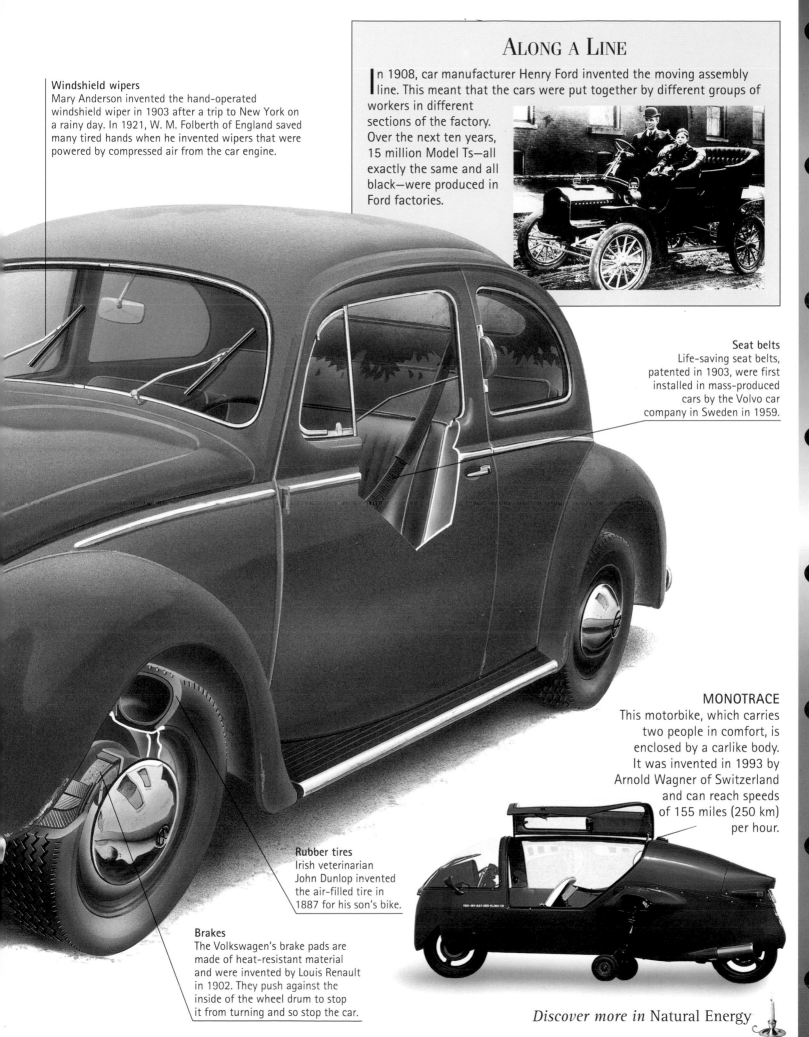

Windshield wipers
Mary Anderson invented the hand-operated windshield wiper in 1903 after a trip to New York on a rainy day. In 1921, W. M. Folberth of England saved many tired hands when he invented wipers that were powered by compressed air from the car engine.

ALONG A LINE

In 1908, car manufacturer Henry Ford invented the moving assembly line. This meant that the cars were put together by different groups of workers in different sections of the factory. Over the next ten years, 15 million Model Ts—all exactly the same and all black—were produced in Ford factories.

Seat belts
Life-saving seat belts, patented in 1903, were first installed in mass-produced cars by the Volvo car company in Sweden in 1959.

MONOTRACE
This motorbike, which carries two people in comfort, is enclosed by a carlike body. It was invented in 1993 by Arnold Wagner of Switzerland and can reach speeds of 155 miles (250 km) per hour.

Rubber tires
Irish veterinarian John Dunlop invented the air-filled tire in 1887 for his son's bike.

Brakes
The Volkswagen's brake pads are made of heat-resistant material and were invented by Louis Renault in 1902. They push against the inside of the wheel drum to stop it from turning and so stop the car.

Discover more in Natural Energy

3200 BC
WHEELED CHARIOT
Mesopotamia

231
WHEELBARROW
China

1861
VELOCIPEDE
Pierre and Ernest Michaux
France

1885
GAS PUMP
Sylvanus Bowser
USA

1885
SPARK PLUGS
Etienne Lenoir
France

1914
ELECTRIC TRAFFIC LIGHT (RED ONLY)
Alfred Benesch
USA

1974
SAFETY AIRBAG
General Motors Corporation
USA

1993
COLLISION AVOIDANCE RADAR
Japan

FINDING THE WAY

Lighthouses can guide ships that are close to shore, but navigation in the open ocean is more difficult. Early sailors relied on the sun, the moon and the stars. Between 850 and 1050, the Chinese invented the magnetic compass to help guide their ships. The mariner's astrolabe (left), and later the sextant and chronometer, made more accurate readings of the heavens possible. Today, ships use satellite signals to navigate.

Safety lines
Ships throughout the world are marked with a Plimsoll line, invented by English politician Samuel Plimsoll in 1876. When a ship is being loaded and the water level reaches the line, it means that no more cargo can be added.

• TRANSPORTATION •

On and Under Water

Boats have a long history. They probably predate the wheel. As early as 40,000 years ago, dugout canoes were paddled across shallow seas. Sails were added by the Egyptians about 5,000 years ago, and the Chinese attached a rudder to the stern for steering about 2,000 years ago. The invention of the steam engine led to the development of bigger, faster and safer ships. Robert Fulton enthralled Americans when he steered his paddle steamer down the Hudson River in 1807. When Isambard Brunel launched his giant steamships in the 1840s, he inspired people everywhere with thoughts of speedy Atlantic crossings. Transport under the sea, however, progressed slowly until the First World War. When the Germans launched their U-boats, submarine warfare was born. Today, undersea vessels are also used for deep-sea salvage and exploration.

CATCHING THE WIND
An exciting new wind sport was created in 1958 when Peter Chilvers of England invented the sailboard. Jim Drake of the United States modified the design and patented it in 1968.

Propeller power
Francis Smith in England and John Ericsson in America invented the screw propeller in the mid-1830s. Propellers were more reliable and could drive ships faster than paddlewheels.

TWO IN ONE
The latest advance on helicopters is the American tiltrotor. It looks like a plane and is just as fast, but it lands and takes off straight up and down like a helicopter.

TIME TO TRAVEL
It would have taken the Wright brothers 138 days to fly around the world in their airplane *Flyer*. Seventy years later, this airbus can circumnavigate the world in 40 hours!

• TRANSPORTATION •

Through the Air

People have wanted to fly since they first saw birds soaring effortlessly through the sky. Many inventors dedicated themselves to discovering the secret of flight. They jumped off high places with feather-covered wings attached to their arms. They built fantastic machines that flapped and fluttered and may have hovered briefly in the air, before crashing to the ground. Kites were first flown by the Chinese philosopher Mo Ti in about 400 BC. In 1783, a hot-air balloon with two French noblemen rose into the skies above Paris. In the 1890s, Clement Ader's steam-powered craft took him to the grand height of 4 inches (10 cm). Wilbur and Orville Wright experimented with aircraft theories and designs for years before their historic flight in 1903.

PAPER BALLOON
The Montgolfier brothers from France built a paper-and-cloth balloon filled with heated air and held together by buttons. A sheep, a duck and a rooster were passengers on its first flight in September, 1783. Two months later, two Frenchmen became the first human passengers in a free-flight balloon.

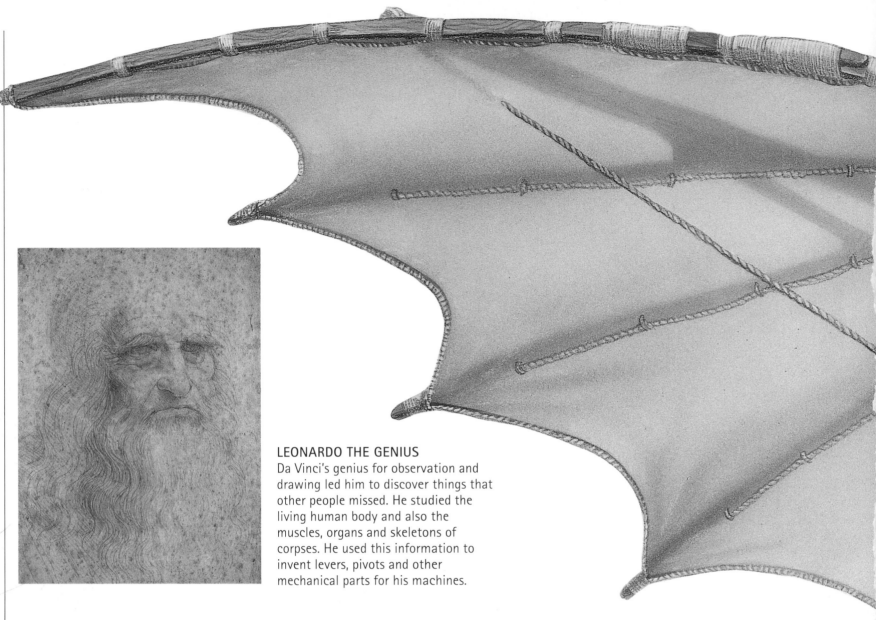

LEONARDO THE GENIUS

Da Vinci's genius for observation and drawing led him to discover things that other people missed. He studied the living human body and also the muscles, organs and skeletons of corpses. He used this information to invent levers, pivots and other mechanical parts for his machines.

• TRANSPORTATION •

Ahead of His Time

Leonardo da Vinci was born in Italy in 1452 during the Renaissance, a time when science, art and invention flourished. Da Vinci was an artist, an architect and above all—a thinker. He had a talent for bringing the future to life in his inventions. He sketched ideas for methods of transportation including the parachute, the life belt, the armored car and even shoes for walking on snow and floating on water. The royal families in Italy asked him for advice about the equipment and strategies they should use in war. Da Vinci's 500-year-old drawings of tools, machines and weapons still look very modern! Many of the inventions he devised, however, were beyond the abilities of the people and technology of the time. Most of his ideas were "re-invented" years after his death.

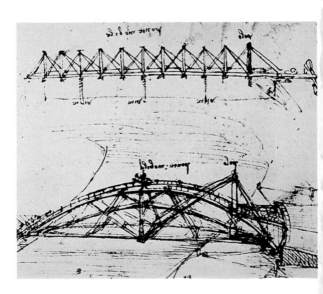

BRIDGES

Leonardo drew an arched bridge that looks remarkably like the Sydney Harbour Bridge in Australia, which was built in 1932.

FLIGHTS OF FANCY
Da Vinci dreamed of learning how to fly by copying the birds. This flapping machine is based on drawings he made in 1505. They show how well he understood the flight of birds.

Sydney Harbour Bridge

SELF-PROPELLED VEHICLE
Leonardo predicted the motor car in this drawing for a self-propelled vehicle, which included the differential, a set of gears that allows the wheels to turn at different speeds to go around corners.

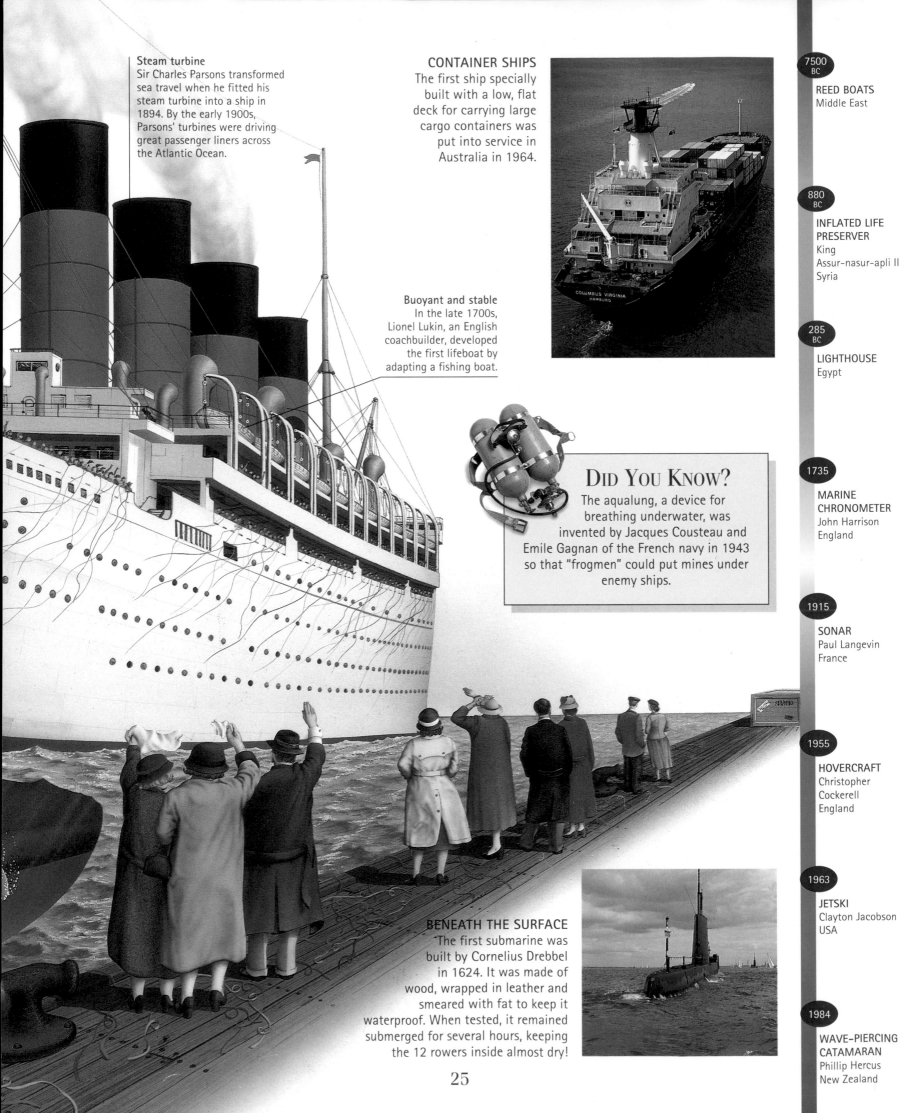

Steam turbine
Sir Charles Parsons transformed sea travel when he fitted his steam turbine into a ship in 1894. By the early 1900s, Parsons' turbines were driving great passenger liners across the Atlantic Ocean.

CONTAINER SHIPS
The first ship specially built with a low, flat deck for carrying large cargo containers was put into service in Australia in 1964.

Buoyant and stable
In the late 1700s, Lionel Lukin, an English coachbuilder, developed the first lifeboat by adapting a fishing boat.

DID YOU KNOW?
The aqualung, a device for breathing underwater, was invented by Jacques Cousteau and Emile Gagnan of the French navy in 1943 so that "frogmen" could put mines under enemy ships.

BENEATH THE SURFACE
The first submarine was built by Cornelius Drebbel in 1624. It was made of wood, wrapped in leather and smeared with fat to keep it waterproof. When tested, it remained submerged for several hours, keeping the 12 rowers inside almost dry!

7500 BC
REED BOATS
Middle East

880 BC
INFLATED LIFE PRESERVER
King Assur-nasur-apli II
Syria

285 BC
LIGHTHOUSE
Egypt

1735
MARINE CHRONOMETER
John Harrison
England

1915
SONAR
Paul Langevin
France

1955
HOVERCRAFT
Christopher Cockerell
England

1963
JETSKI
Clayton Jacobson
USA

1984
WAVE-PIERCING CATAMARAN
Phillip Hercus
New Zealand

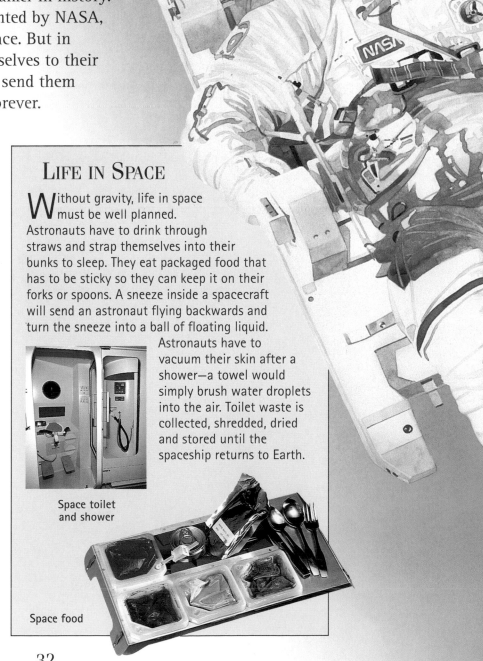

To Outer Space

S pace is a dangerous place. There is no air, no food, no sound and no gravity. Without a spaceship or a spacesuit to provide air pressure, your body would explode into billions of tiny pieces. The Italian mathematician and astronomer Galileo Galilei saw the surface of the moon through a telescope in 1609. People soon began to dream of reaching such a wondrous place. In 1965, American astronauts "walked" in space wearing shiny, airtight, water-cooled spacesuits, helmets and oxygen tanks. They were attached to their spaceship by ropes. Four years later, *Apollo 11* landed on the moon and Neil Armstrong became the most famous moonwalker in history. *Apollo 11* astronauts had personal jetpacks, invented by NASA, to help them travel quickly over the moon's surface. But in space, they had to tie themselves to their spacecraft—a jetpack could send them spinning into deep space forever.

ROCKET MAN
In 1926, an American professor, Robert Goddard, invented a liquid-fueled rocket. It flew to a height of only 44 ft (13.5 m) before it crash-landed. Ten years passed before scientists paid any attention to his invention.

LIFE IN SPACE

W ithout gravity, life in space must be well planned. Astronauts have to drink through straws and strap themselves into their bunks to sleep. They eat packaged food that has to be sticky so they can keep it on their forks or spoons. A sneeze inside a spacecraft will send an astronaut flying backwards and turn the sneeze into a ball of floating liquid.

Astronauts have to vacuum their skin after a shower—a towel would simply brush water droplets into the air. Toilet waste is collected, shredded, dried and stored until the spaceship returns to Earth.

Space toilet and shower

MOON BUGGY
The Lunar Rover, invented by the Boeing company in 1971, was the first car in space. It could speed across the moon at 37 miles (60 km) per hour, and could be completely folded up and stored in the spaceship.

Space food

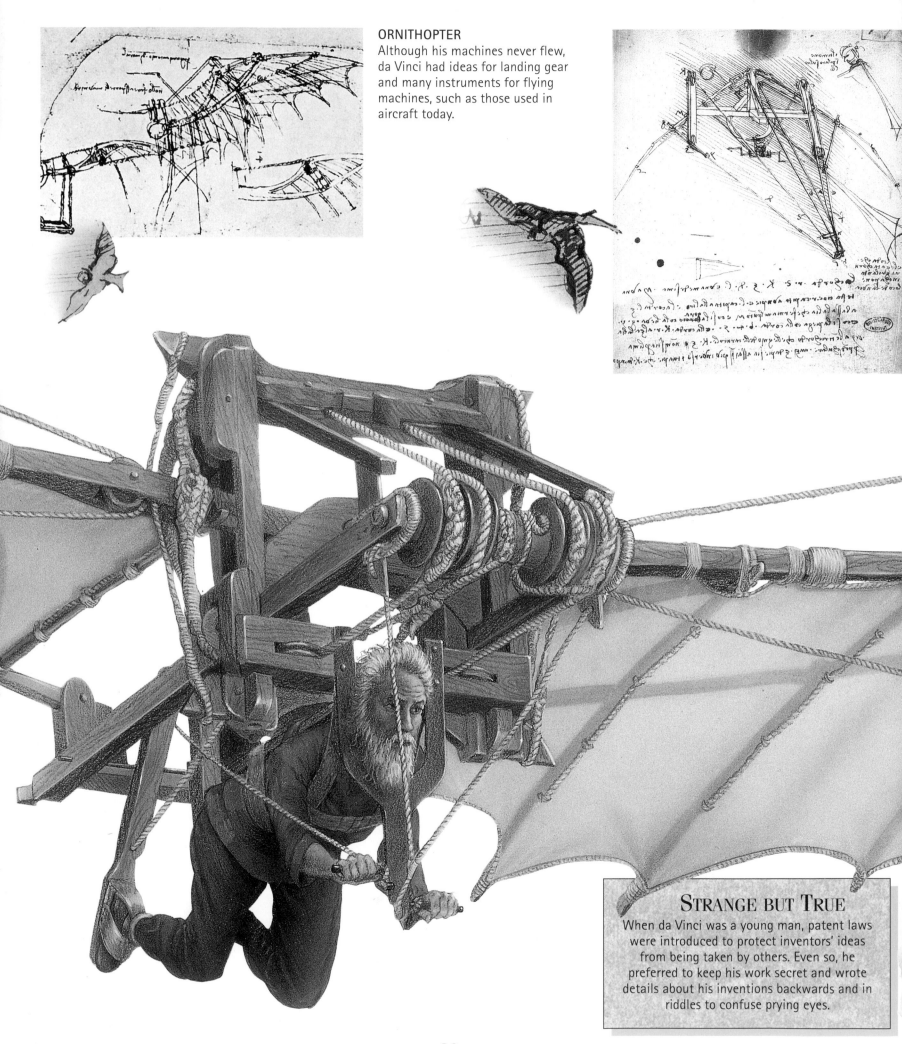

ORNITHOPTER
Although his machines never flew, da Vinci had ideas for landing gear and many instruments for flying machines, such as those used in aircraft today.

STRANGE BUT TRUE
When da Vinci was a young man, patent laws were introduced to protect inventors' ideas from being taken by others. Even so, he preferred to keep his work secret and wrote details about his inventions backwards and in riddles to confuse prying eyes.

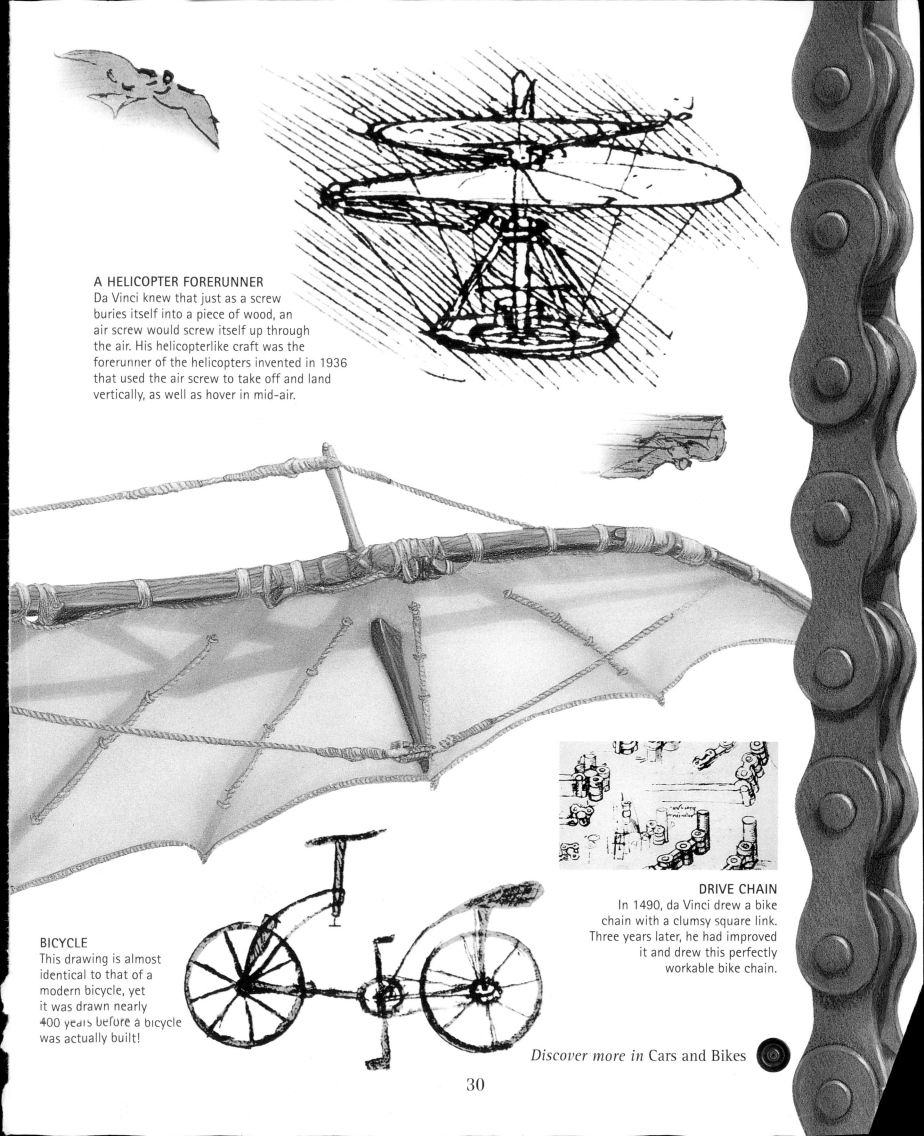

A HELICOPTER FORERUNNER
Da Vinci knew that just as a screw buries itself into a piece of wood, an air screw would screw itself up through the air. His helicopterlike craft was the forerunner of the helicopters invented in 1936 that used the air screw to take off and land vertically, as well as hover in mid-air.

BICYCLE
This drawing is almost identical to that of a modern bicycle, yet it was drawn nearly 400 years before a bicycle was actually built!

DRIVE CHAIN
In 1490, da Vinci drew a bike chain with a clumsy square link. Three years later, he had improved it and drew this perfectly workable bike chain.

Discover more in Cars and Bikes

A VIEW FROM ABOVE
From about 400 BC, the Chinese supposedly sent people up in kites to survey activity on the ground.

AIRSHIPS
A huge, rigid (framed) balloon with motors was invented in 1900 by Count Ferdinand von Zeppelin. It was filled with hydrogen gas, which is highly explosive and caused some terrible fires on airships. When the famous *Hindenberg* burst into flames on landing in 1937, the airship age ended.

THE WRIGHT BROTHERS

In 1903, at Kitty Hawk beach in North Carolina, Americans Orville and Wilbur Wright tossed a coin to decide who would fly their carefully constructed biplane. Wilbur almost became the first pilot in the world, but the engine of the *Flyer* spluttered and the plane crashed into the sand. Orville Wright was luckier. He flew 169 ft (51.5 m) in just over ten seconds—the first powered flight and an inspiration to inventors of airplanes everywhere.

Discover more in Ahead of His Time

31

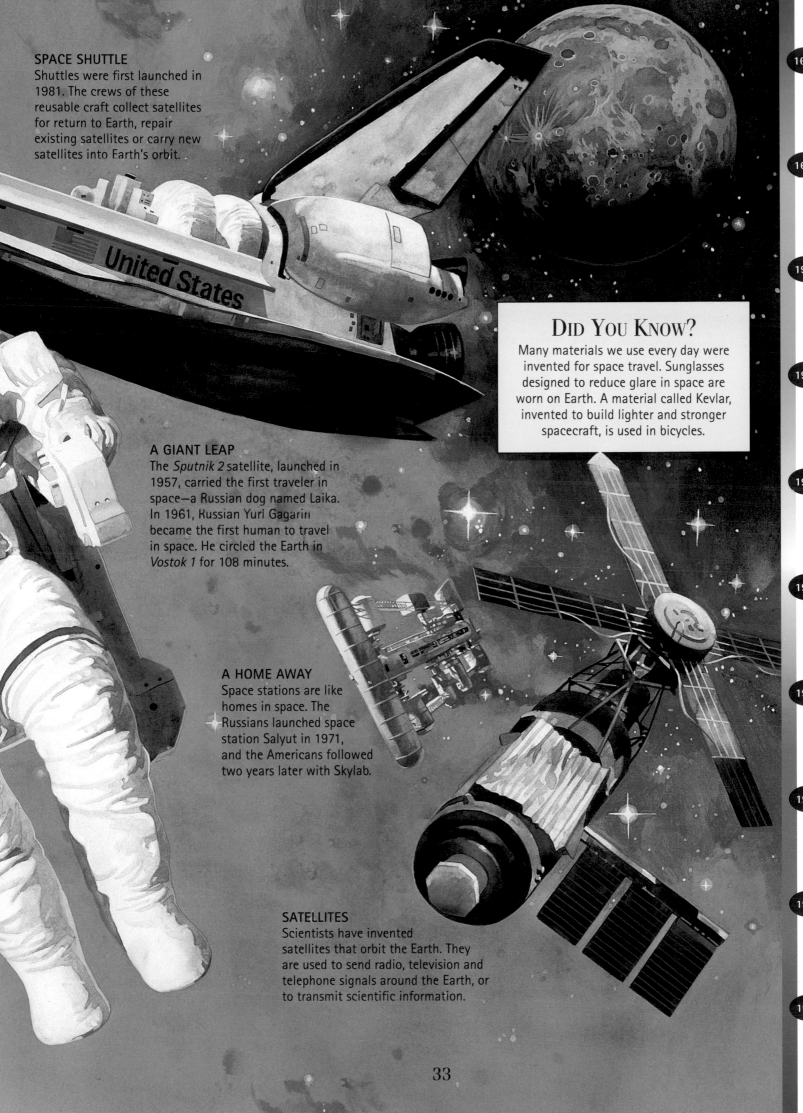

SPACE SHUTTLE

Shuttles were first launched in 1981. The crews of these reusable craft collect satellites for return to Earth, repair existing satellites or carry new satellites into Earth's orbit.

DID YOU KNOW?

Many materials we use every day were invented for space travel. Sunglasses designed to reduce glare in space are worn on Earth. A material called Kevlar, invented to build lighter and stronger spacecraft, is used in bicycles.

A GIANT LEAP

The *Sputnik 2* satellite, launched in 1957, carried the first traveler in space—a Russian dog named Laika. In 1961, Russian Yuri Gagarin became the first human to travel in space. He circled the Earth in *Vostok 1* for 108 minutes.

A HOME AWAY

Space stations are like homes in space. The Russians launched space station Salyut in 1971, and the Americans followed two years later with Skylab.

SATELLITES

Scientists have invented satellites that orbit the Earth. They are used to send radio, television and telephone signals around the Earth, or to transmit scientific information.

1608
TELESCOPE
Hans Lippershey
Netherlands

1668
REFLECTING
TELESCOPE
Isaac Newton
England

1926
LIQUID-FUELED
ROCKET
Robert Goddard
USA

1932
RADIO TELESCOPE
Karl Jansky
USA

1942
V2 ROCKET
Dornberger, Theil
and von Braun
Germany

1957
SPUTNIK 1
Dr Sergei Korolyov
USSR

1969
APOLLO 11
NASA
USA

1981
SPACE SHUTTLE
NASA
USA

1989
GALILEO SPACE
PROBE
NASA
USA

1990
HUBBLE SPACE
TELESCOPE
NASA
USA

33

REED PEN
A hollow reed can be cut to a point and used as a pen with ink or paint.

PENCIL
In 1792, Jacques Nicolas Conté invented a hard, long-wearing pencil made from clay mixed with powdered graphite and covered in cedar wood.

HIEROGLYPHS
The Egyptians developed a type of picture writing called hieroglyphs about 3000 BC. They either carved these pictures into stone, or painted them onto walls or papyrus with a pen cut from a reed from the River Nile.

FOUNTAIN PEN
This pen, which stores ink in its handle, was invented in 1884 by American Lewis Waterman.

CALLIGRAPHY BRUSH
This is used by trained writers, called calligraphers, to paint words onto rice paper and silk.

BALLPOINT PEN
In 1938, Laszlo Biro from Hungary invented a pen that used a rolling ball instead of a nib.

SEAL OF APPROVAL
A seal is a device used to imprint a design or symbol that represents a family or a company. The first seals were used in Sumeria and India for signing documents.

• COMMUNICATIONS •

From Quill to Press

Technology has made it possible for us to communicate in different ways. People all over the world write with pens and pencils; many key their words into computers. About 30,000 years ago, however, people drew pictures on cave walls to tell stories or record news. The ancient Sumerians replaced this form of picture writing with shapes that they pressed into wet clay. The Chinese invented 50,000 characters that were written onto paper or silk with a brush. The first books in Europe were written with ink and a quill—a feather plucked from a goose and cut to a sharp point. The Chinese printed books by using wooden blocks. Later, they created movable, fire-baked characters that could be dipped into ink and pressed onto paper, but they wore out quickly. This problem was solved by the invention of reusable type made of hard metal. The printing press was soon in operation.

THE PRINTING PRESS

German printer Johannes Gutenberg developed a printing press with movable type around 1447. Seven years later, he printed the first Latin edition of the Bible. Gutenberg had worked on his invention in secret and borrowed money to help pay his costs. But he could not repay his loan and had to give away his movable type. By 1460, however, Gutenberg had managed to start a new printing business.

TYPE BLOCKS
Gutenberg made metal type molds of each letter. They were set one by one into pages held together in a wooden frame.

Paper press
Gutenberg used a huge wooden screw to press paper onto the inked type.

Paper bed
This held the printed paper while it dried.

Ink for printing
Gutenberg invented special "sticky" oil-based ink. One application could print up to ten pages.

Type bed
The wooden frame that held the type blocks was placed on the stone, or bed, of the press.

30,000 BC
CAVE PAINTINGS
Europe

2600 BC
INK FOR PAPYRUS
Egypt, China

105
PAPER
(MULBERRY)
Cai Lun
China

500
GOOSE-FEATHER
QUILL
Europe

868
FIRST PRINTED
BOOK
Buddhist priests
China

1447
GUTENBERG PRESS
Johannes Gutenberg
Germany

1609
NEWSPAPER
Julius Sohne
Germany

1886
KEYBOARD TYPE
SETTING
Ottmar Mergenthaler
USA

35

FIBER OPTICS

In 1976, the Western Electric Company of Atlanta, Georgia used pulses of laser light to send voice, video and computer messages through fibers made of glass, which were called optical fibers.

EXCHANGING WORDS

As a telephone wire could carry only one message at a time, Bell and Gray invented the telephone exchange system in 1878. Within ten years, hundreds of wires connected houses to buildings called exchanges, where operators joined the wires so that people could speak to each other.

MAKING CONNECTIONS

On February 14, 1876, Scottish-born Alexander Graham Bell and American Elisha Gray both applied to patent the telephone in the United States, although neither of them had made a telephone that really worked. Gray was two hours later than Bell and lost the race to claim the telephone as his invention. People were very eager to invest in this exciting new technology, and by the end of 1877, Bell was a millionaire.

ELECTRIC TELEGRAPH

In 1837, the American Samuel Morse used a magnet to interrupt the flow of electricity in a wire. This could be heard at the other end of the wire as a "beep." The beeps were formed into a code (Morse code) that operators learned to understand and translate back into words.

CANDLESTICK TELEPHONE

This was the most common telephone in the world for many years. The early models did not have dials, and you had to rattle the side hook to alert the operator. Frenchman Antoine Barnay invented the dial in 1923.

• COMMUNICATIONS •

Along a Wire

Messages can be passed from person to person in many ways. Voices, horns and beating drums carry messages through the air; written messages are sent by mail. All early methods of communication relied on how far people could run, see, hear or shout. The first messages to travel further and faster were sent by telegraph in the 1830s. The telegraph consisted of a special code of electric "beeps" that traveled huge distances along wires in a few minutes. At the other end, the receiver sorted the beeps into words and delivered the message in person. In 1851, the first telegraph cable was laid under the English Channel between Dover and Calais. By 1866, undersea cables provided the first transatlantic telecommunications link. Today, wires still connect millions of people by telephone, fax and computer.

DID YOU KNOW?
You can make a string telephone by connecting two containers, or cans, by a long length of string. Pull the string tight and speak into one container. The person at the other end should be able to hear what you say. Children have made string telephones since the 1600s.

1832–1837
ELECTRIC TELEGRAPH SYSTEMS
Faraday/Schilling
England, Russia

1837
MORSE ELECTRIC TELEGRAPH
Samuel Morse
USA

1851
UNDERWATER CABLE
Charles Wheatstone and Joseph Brett
England

1889
PUBLIC TELEPHONE
William Gray
USA

1895
WIRELESS TELEGRAPH
Guglielmo Marconi
Italy

1903
PHOTO–TELEGRAPH
Arthur Korn
Germany

1916
TELEX
Markrum Company
USA

1955
OPTICAL FIBER
Dr Narinder Kapany
England

WIRED FOR SOUND

The electric microphone, which amplifies, or increases, sound, was invented in 1916 and first tested at Madison Square Gardens, New York.

HEADPHONES

These were developed from hearing-aid technology invented in 1901 by American Miller Hutchinson.

• COMMUNICATIONS •

Pictures and Sound

People told stories and cast shadow shapes on the walls of firelit caves thousands of years ago. In the 1640s they used early projectors called "magic lanterns" to shine candlelight through hand-painted glass slides. Frenchman Gaspard Robert invented the marvellous Fantasmagoria in 1798. This special kind of magic lantern projected moving pictures and shadows of ghosts and monsters onto sheets in a dark room. Audiences screamed and fainted at the sight, and quickly lined up to see it all over again. In 1891, the brilliant American inventor Thomas Edison developed a moving-picture camera called a Kinetograph and opened the way for silent movies and stars of the screen such as Charlie Chaplin. Within the next 40 years, inventions such as radio, television, film and video brought new dimensions to the quality of pictures and sound.

PUMPING THE PIANO

The Fotoplayer Company of Berkeley, California invented the Fotoplayer in 1915. This huge piano was powered by an air pump and played music programmed by a roll of punched paper. It provided sound effects for silent movies.

Light-activated sound strip

RADIO

In 1906, Reginald Fessenden broadcast voice and music on radio waves for the first time.

TIMING SOUND

Phonograph records added lifelike sound to movies. But it was difficult to match the record with the action on the movie; voices often finished after the actors had stopped mouthing the words. In the 1929 movie *Hallelujah*, sound was recorded as a pattern on the film. This pattern was "read" by a light-sensitive cell that synchronized sound with the moving pictures.

PICTURES TO EUROPE

In 1962, the first television pictures were sent from the United States to Europe. They bounced off the *Telstar* satellite in space and were collected by a dish-shaped antenna like this.

BOX "BROWNIE" CAMERA

In 1888, George Eastman invented the roll-film camera. In 1900, he developed the box "brownie" model. It sold for US 50 cents, which included the film and the developing.

COMPACT DISC

Japanese and Dutch scientists invented the CD in 1981. It records sounds as microscopic changes in the surface of a plastic disc. The changes are "read" by a laser in the CD player and changed back into sound electronically.

JOHN LOGIE BAIRD

Mechanical television was invented by the Scottish engineer John Logie Baird in 1923. His television was a combination of inventions and discoveries by other people. Baird's cameras and receivers contained a spinning disc invented by Nipkow of Germany in 1884. The disc translated pictures into dots of light in eight lines that were focused onto a tiny television screen.

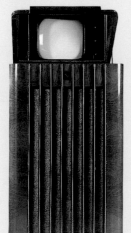

1939 German television

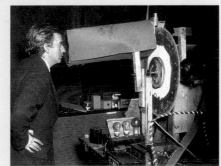

John Logie Baird and the first TV transmitter

TWO FOR ONE

The video camera was invented in America in 1931, but it was larger than a human and could only send pictures, not record them. In 1981, the Sony Corporation of Japan invented a hand-held video camera that records as well.

1640

MAGIC LANTERN
Athanase Kircher
Germany

1827

PHOTOGRAPH
Joseph Nicéphore
Niepce
France

1877

WHEEL OF LIFE
ANIMATOR
Emile Raynaud
France

1895

RADIO
TELEGRAPH
Guglielmo Marconi
Italy

1906

FEATURE FILM
Charles and John
Tait
Australia

1931

ELECTRONIC
TELEVISION
Vladimir Zworykin
USA

1962

SATELLITE
TELEVISION
Telstar
USA

1980

WALKMAN™ TAPE
PLAYER
Ako Morita
Japan

2000?

3-D TELEVISION

Reed
The reed is a thin piece of wood or metal inside the mouthpiece.

SAXOPHONE
Adolphe Sax of Belgium invented the saxophone in 1841. He patented it in 1846 and spent the next 11 years practicing and studying before teaching students at the Paris Conservatoire.

Musical Instruments

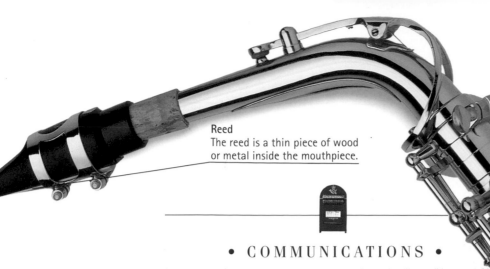

Sounds are made by waves or vibrations of air. The first musical instrument was the human voice. When we sing, the air in our throat vibrates. It echoes around our mouth and nose and, hopefully, comes out as music. The first musicians learned to use objects such as shells to make their voices louder, and soon realized that musical sounds could be made by plucking the string of a hunting bow or blowing into an animal bone. Most musical instruments have evolved through the tiny improvements made by instrument makers year after year. The first wind instruments were simple animal-bone flutes; stringed instruments, such as the harp, developed into the violin and the piano. Computers now enable us to create a wide variety of sounds electronically without blowing, hitting, plucking or strumming anything at all. Music can be made by everyone.

Keys
Mechanical keys for wind instruments were invented in the 1800s by the German instrument maker Theobald Boëhm.

GUITAR
A type of guitar was played in the Middle East from about 1000 BC. The modern acoustic guitar was invented in 1850 by Antonio de Torres, a Spanish instrument maker.

INDONESIAN GAMELAN ORCHESTRA
These players use mainly percussion instruments, including the saron and bonang, to play the melody by heart. They use string instruments such as the rebab and chelempung to enhance the sound.

PAN FLUTE
The first flutes were made from the hollow bones of sheep. Leg bones were punched with holes that were covered by the fingers to alter the pitch of the notes.

PLAYING THE PIANO
In 1710, Italian Bartolommeo Christofori invented keys attached to small hammers to strike strings. He called his invention the "piano-forte," which means soft and loud.

PLAYING PERCUSSION
This Chinese instrument dates back to about 1000 BC. Different-sized sheets of metal were hung on a frame and struck with a wooden mallet.

BEATING TIME
No one knows who made the first drum. These African drums have animal skin stretched over one end, which the player hits to produce a sound.

NOTATING MUSIC
Greek scholars first wrote down music in 500 BC as a line of alphabetical signs. The signs showed musicians if a note should be played high or low. Symbols called "neumes," which stood for notes or groups of notes, were introduced in AD 650. In 1026, Italian Guido d'Arezzo introduced a system whereby the neumes were placed high or low on a line to show the pitch of the note. Rhythm and timing were added in about 1500.

15th-century music score

Original Handel score

5000 BC
DIDGERIDOO
Australia

3000 BC
HARP
Sumeria, Egypt

220 BC
PIPE ORGAN
Ctesibius
Alexandria

1300
HARPSICORD
Europe

1816
METRONOME
Johann Maelzel
Germany

1821
HARMONICA
C. F. L. Buschmann
Germany

1935
ELECTRIC GUITAR
Rickenbacher
USA

1965
SYNTHESIZER
Robert Moog
USA

41

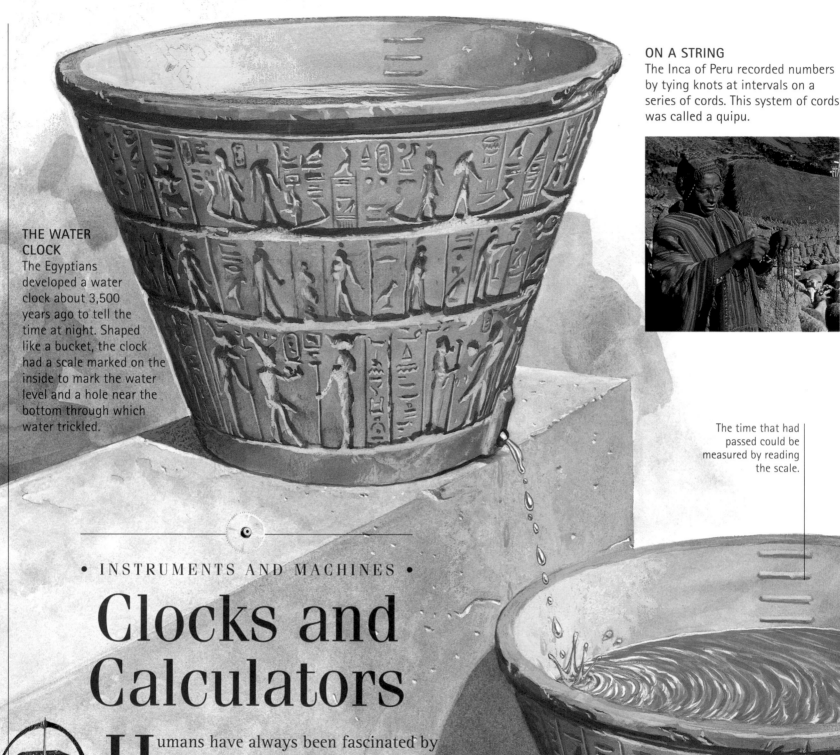

THE WATER CLOCK
The Egyptians developed a water clock about 3,500 years ago to tell the time at night. Shaped like a bucket, the clock had a scale marked on the inside to mark the water level and a hole near the bottom through which water trickled.

The time that had passed could be measured by reading the scale.

• INSTRUMENTS AND MACHINES •

Clocks and Calculators

Humans have always been fascinated by time. The first clocks used natural rhythms such as the movement of the sun to measure time. Later, the desire to divide up the day more precisely led to the invention of mechanical clocks. Powered by the energy stored in a metal spring, or weights on a chain, these clocks relied on an important device called the escapement, which turned the energy into a regular movement. By the mid-1600s, the accuracy of clockwork cogs and gears had caught the attention of mathematicians, and counting machines were invented to take the hard work out of sums. Inventors everywhere were inspired by the mechanical clock. They imagined that clockwork could be used to power all their wonderful ideas for the future.

42

THE MECHANICAL CALCULATOR

In 1642, 19-year-old Blaise Pascal built a simple arithmetic machine for his father, whose job involved counting money. The machine used clockwork gears to automatically add (up to eight-digit figures) or subtract. Some years later, a great mathematician, Gottfried Leibniz, developed Pascal's machine into a new model that could add, subtract, multiply, divide and find the square root of numbers. This was the starting point for all true calculators, and eventually, computers.

MARKING TIME

Inspired by the action of a church lamp swinging steadily during an earth tremor, Italian Galileo Galilei invented the pendulum in 1581. The first pendulum clock was made in 1656 by a Dutch scientist, Christiaan Huygens.

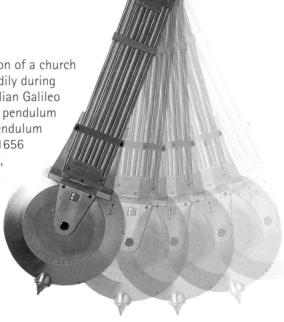

KEEPING THE CHANGE

In 1879, American James Ritty invented the cash register to discourage his bar staff from stealing the profits. The register used a clockwork mechanism to add, total and print transactions.

PLOTTING THE HEAVENS

The orrery is a clockwork model that shows the movements of planets around the sun. It was named after the English Earl of Orrery who had the first one built in about 1720.

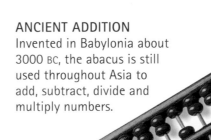

ANCIENT ADDITION

Invented in Babylonia about 3000 BC, the abacus is still used throughout Asia to add, subtract, divide and multiply numbers.

3400 BC
NUMBERS
Middle East

3000 BC
ABACUS
Babylonia

400
CANDLE AND FUSE CLOCK
Byzantium

725?
ESCAPEMENT
I. Hing
China

1335
CHIMING CLOCK
Italy

1624
CLOCKWORK CALCULATOR
Wilhelm Schickard
Germany

1840
ELECTRIC CLOCK
Alexander Bain
England

1847
ALARM CLOCK
Antoine Redier
France

1907
MODERN WRISTWATCH
Louis Cartier and
Hans Wilsdorf
France, Switzerland

1948
ATOMIC CLOCK
Frank Libby
USA

Computers and Robots

A SLAVE TO THE JOB
The word robot comes from the Czech "robotnik," which means "work slave." A robot can do many things faster and better than humans can.

Two hundred years ago, people who figured out, or computed, difficult mathematical problems were called "computers." Today, computers are machines that use electronic circuits to store information such as numbers, words, pictures, sounds, shapes and calculations in code. Computers are used to control the most complex tools that have been invented—robots. These sophisticated machines are faster, more accurate and stronger than people. They can work in places and conditions where people could not survive, and they do not get bored doing the same thing every day! Virtual reality is a new invention that uses technology in a unique way. Special helmets, gloves and sensors connect a person's sight, hearing and touch to a computer. In the future, virtual reality will enable surgeons in one country to perform an operation in another country.

LAPTOP COMPUTER
In 1987, Clive Sinclair of England invented a portable, or laptop, computer that weighed less than 2 pounds (1 kg).

SILICON CHIPS
Microscopic electrical circuits etched into chips of silicon were invented in 1959 by American Jack Kilby. These wafers hold hundreds of tiny silicon chips—each one powerful enough to run a small computer.

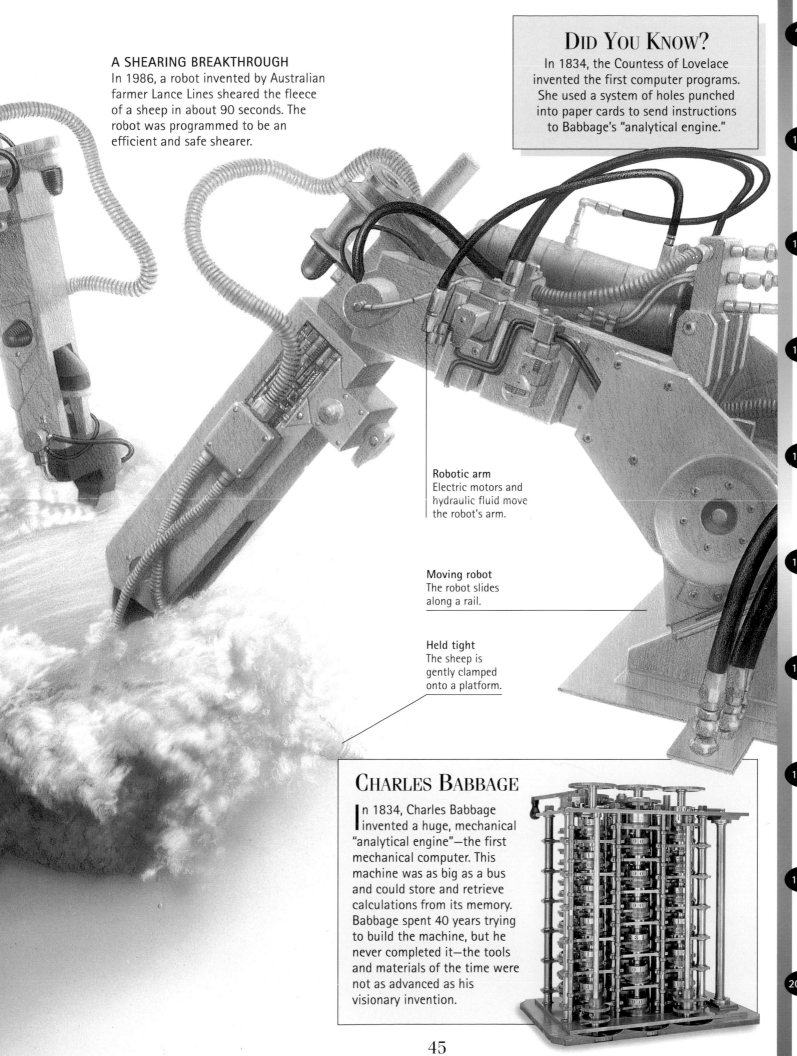

A SHEARING BREAKTHROUGH
In 1986, a robot invented by Australian farmer Lance Lines sheared the fleece of a sheep in about 90 seconds. The robot was programmed to be an efficient and safe shearer.

DID YOU KNOW?
In 1834, the Countess of Lovelace invented the first computer programs. She used a system of holes punched into paper cards to send instructions to Babbage's "analytical engine."

Robotic arm
Electric motors and hydraulic fluid move the robot's arm.

Moving robot
The robot slides along a rail.

Held tight
The sheep is gently clamped onto a platform.

CHARLES BABBAGE
In 1834, Charles Babbage invented a huge, mechanical "analytical engine"—the first mechanical computer. This machine was as big as a bus and could store and retrieve calculations from its memory. Babbage spent 40 years trying to build the machine, but he never completed it—the tools and materials of the time were not as advanced as his visionary invention.

400 BC
AUTOMATON
Archytas of Tarentum
Greece

1834
ANALYTICAL ENGINE
Charles Babbage
England

1859
BINARY LOGIC
George Boole
England

1907
AUTOMATIC TOTALIZATOR
George Julius
Australia

1941
COLOSSUS COMPUTER
Neuman and Turing
England

1954
COMMERCIAL MAGNETIC MEMORY COMPUTER
IBM
USA

1962
COMMERCIAL ROBOTICS
Unimation
USA

1975
PERSONAL COMPUTER
H. Edward Roberts
USA

1985
CD-ROM
Philips/Hitachi
Netherlands, Japan

2000?
VIRTUAL SURGERY

45

Early Power

Hero, a mathematician in ancient Alexandria, first used steam power to make a metal ball spin. But he considered his invention a toy. More than 1,600 years later, inventors experimented with steam power again, but this time, the results of their efforts revolutionized people's lives. In the 1700s and 1800s, the steam-powered engine was adapted to do almost everything: pump water, drive factory machinery, propel ships, plow fields and even drive fairground rides. Some of the early steamships made so much smoke and noise that people were very reluctant to travel on them! The age of steam lasted for almost 200 years until the internal-combustion engine and electricity took over. Steam, however, is not as old-fashioned as you might think. Most of the electricity that gives us power today is produced by huge, steam-driven machines called turbines.

STRANGE BUT TRUE

Henry Seely of New York was ahead of his time. He invented the electric iron in 1882, but he could not sell it because nobody had electricity in their houses!

SMOOTHING OUT THE BUMPS
Without the steamroller, invented by Frenchman Louis Lemoine in 1859, roads would never have been smooth enough for the first fragile cars.

EDISON AND THE LIGHT BULB

In the late 1800s, people predicted that electricity would be the power source of the future. Thomas Edison based his greatest inventions on electric power. In ten years he invented the electric light, an improved electric engine and generator, and a storage battery. In 1880, he opened the first power stations in London and New York to provide electric lighting.

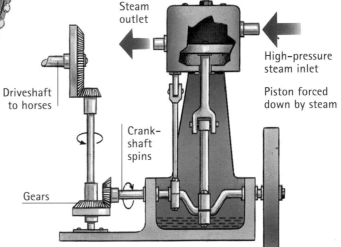

Steam outlet

High-pressure steam inlet

Piston forced down by steam

Driveshaft to horses

Crank-shaft spins

Gears

STEAM POWER
The steam for most engines was heated by burning coal or wood. The pressure of the steam from the engine above pushed a piston up and down, turning the shaft that moved the horses.

POWER FOR THE FACTORY
In 1785, James Watt invented a steam engine that could power a whole factory of machines from its single revolving shaft. The output of his engine was measured in horsepower, for the number of horses it replaced.

47

1690
STEAM CYLINDER ENGINE
Denis Papin
France

1698
STEAM PUMP
Thomas Savery
England

1705
ENGINE WITH BOILER
Thomas Newcomen
England

1730
STEAMBOAT
Jonathan Hulls
England

1800
VOLTAIC CELL
Allesandro Volta
Italy

1821
ELECTRIC MOTOR
Michael Faraday
England

1829
STEAM PLOW
USA

1878
ELECTRIC DC GENERATOR
Thomas Edison
USA

1882
ALTERNATING CURRENT GENERATOR
Nikola Tesla
USA

1884
STEAM-POWERED TURBINE
Charles Parsons
England

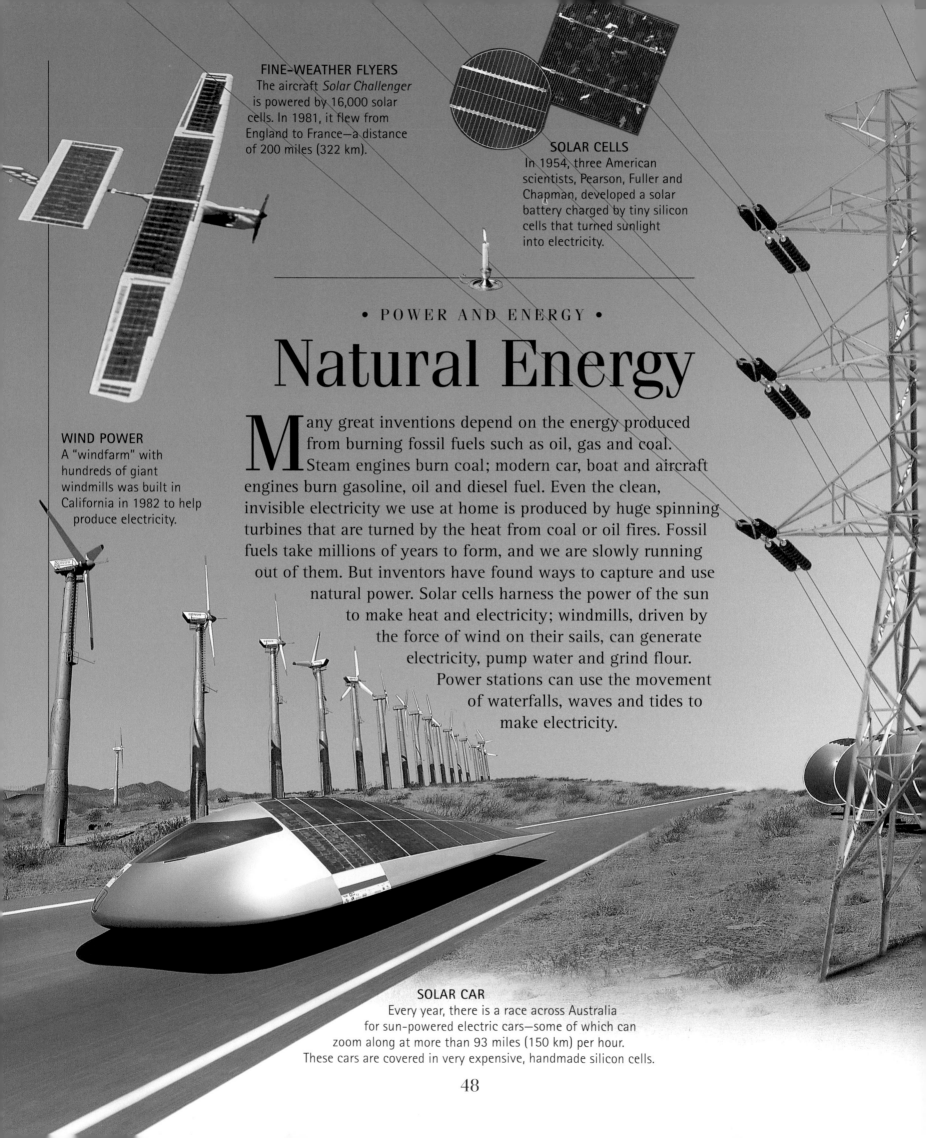

FINE-WEATHER FLYERS
The aircraft *Solar Challenger* is powered by 16,000 solar cells. In 1981, it flew from England to France—a distance of 200 miles (322 km).

SOLAR CELLS
In 1954, three American scientists, Pearson, Fuller and Chapman, developed a solar battery charged by tiny silicon cells that turned sunlight into electricity.

• POWER AND ENERGY •

Natural Energy

Many great inventions depend on the energy produced from burning fossil fuels such as oil, gas and coal. Steam engines burn coal; modern car, boat and aircraft engines burn gasoline, oil and diesel fuel. Even the clean, invisible electricity we use at home is produced by huge spinning turbines that are turned by the heat from coal or oil fires. Fossil fuels take millions of years to form, and we are slowly running out of them. But inventors have found ways to capture and use natural power. Solar cells harness the power of the sun to make heat and electricity; windmills, driven by the force of wind on their sails, can generate electricity, pump water and grind flour. Power stations can use the movement of waterfalls, waves and tides to make electricity.

WIND POWER
A "windfarm" with hundreds of giant windmills was built in California in 1982 to help produce electricity.

SOLAR CAR
Every year, there is a race across Australia for sun-powered electric cars—some of which can zoom along at more than 93 miles (150 km) per hour. These cars are covered in very expensive, handmade silicon cells.

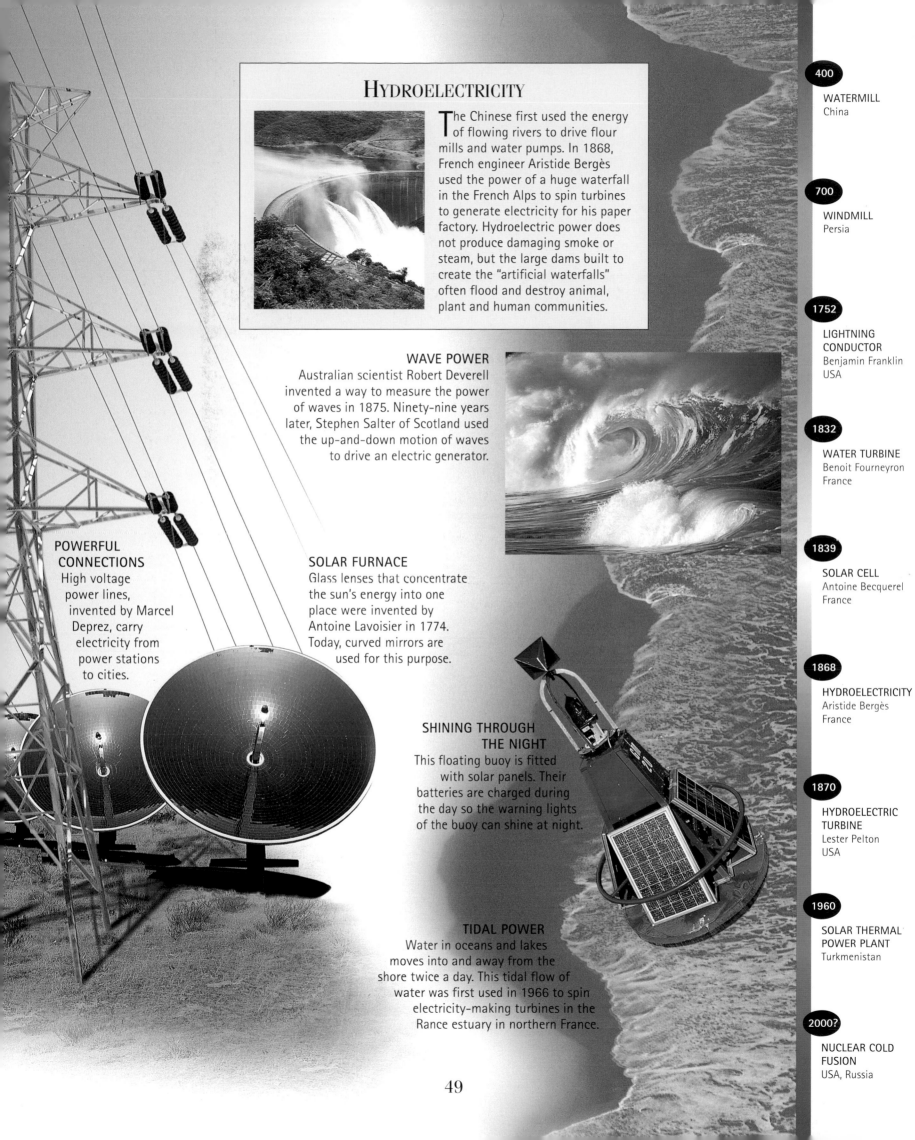

HYDROELECTRICITY

The Chinese first used the energy of flowing rivers to drive flour mills and water pumps. In 1868, French engineer Aristide Bergès used the power of a huge waterfall in the French Alps to spin turbines to generate electricity for his paper factory. Hydroelectric power does not produce damaging smoke or steam, but the large dams built to create the "artificial waterfalls" often flood and destroy animal, plant and human communities.

WAVE POWER

Australian scientist Robert Deverell invented a way to measure the power of waves in 1875. Ninety-nine years later, Stephen Salter of Scotland used the up-and-down motion of waves to drive an electric generator.

POWERFUL CONNECTIONS

High voltage power lines, invented by Marcel Deprez, carry electricity from power stations to cities.

SOLAR FURNACE

Glass lenses that concentrate the sun's energy into one place were invented by Antoine Lavoisier in 1774. Today, curved mirrors are used for this purpose.

SHINING THROUGH THE NIGHT

This floating buoy is fitted with solar panels. Their batteries are charged during the day so the warning lights of the buoy can shine at night.

TIDAL POWER

Water in oceans and lakes moves into and away from the shore twice a day. This tidal flow of water was first used in 1966 to spin electricity-making turbines in the Rance estuary in northern France.

49

400
WATERMILL
China

700
WINDMILL
Persia

1752
LIGHTNING CONDUCTOR
Benjamin Franklin
USA

1832
WATER TURBINE
Benoit Fourneyron
France

1839
SOLAR CELL
Antoine Becquerel
France

1868
HYDROELECTRICITY
Aristide Bergès
France

1870
HYDROELECTRIC TURBINE
Lester Pelton
USA

1960
SOLAR THERMAL POWER PLANT
Turkmenistan

2000?
NUCLEAR COLD FUSION
USA, Russia

DEADLY BEAUTY
This razor-sharp sword was used by Japanese Samurai warriors to kill their enemy in one blow. Invented around 1200, a Samurai sword is made from up to 20 layers of steel beaten together. It is then sharpened until it can split a human hair in half.

BOW AND ARROW
The English longbow, invented in about 1330, was very accurate and could kill an enemy 1,640 ft (500 m) away.

• WAR AND PEACE •

Into Battle

The history of the world is full of stories of war. Many inventions were developed especially as weapons to be used in battle. Clubs, axes and swords were wielded in the hand-to-hand combat of early wars. In the third century BC, the Greek scholar Archimedes gave soldiers curved and polished shields to reflect the sun into the eyes of Romans invading the city of Syracuse. People still fight with wooden shields in New Guinea. A European knight in the 1500s rode into battle covered from top to toe in metal armor that protected him from the swords, arrows, axes and spears of his enemies. His horse was also covered in menacing armor. But if the knight fell or was knocked from his horse, the weight of the armor made it difficult for him to stand and defend himself. He became an easy target for enemy knights.

BATTLE-AX
Copper axes were first invented in Mesopotamia in 4000 BC, probably as a hand tool, but they soon became weapons. This is a Viking battle-ax from the thirteenth century.

50

CHINESE MILITARY ROCKET
Simple rockets were invented in 1100 in China. These rockets exploded into flames when they landed.

DID YOU KNOW?
An old form of flexible armor called chain mail has found new uses today. Butchers wear chain mail gloves to protect their hands, and divers wear chain mail suits to protect them against sharks.

SHIELD OF HONOUR
A shield was more than a protective device. It was often decorated with patterns to represent the family or tribe of the person using it.

CANNONS AND GUNPOWDER
Gunpowder was first invented around AD 850 by chemists in China. They used it in fireworks, but later it became popular as an explosive in China, India and Europe. The first gun was a metal firing tube made in Europe in about 1300 by a monk. Cannons were invented in Italy at about the same time, but they produced a spray of iron bullets and did not always hit their target. In the 1500s, the first accurate cannons were invented in France. Warfare took a new turn.

Discover more in Today and Tomorrow

500,000 BC
SPEAR
Europe

230,000 BC
STONE AX
Kenya

30,000 BC
BOW AND ARROW
Africa, USA, Europe

3000 BC
SWORD
Mesopotamia

500 BC
CATAPULT
Greece

400 BC
CHAIN MAIL ARMOR
Italy

300 BC
HAND-HELD CROSSBOW
China

850
BLACK GUNPOWDER
China

Today and Tomorrow

Technological progress is faster in times of war. Each side tries to make weapons and machines that are bigger and better than those of the enemy. At the beginning of the First World War, for example, the typical flying speed of an airplane was 70 miles (113 km) per hour. By the end of the war this speed had doubled. In the Second World War, the Germans introduced two inventions that later transformed flight—the turbojet, which became the basis of modern aircraft, and the ballistic missile, which took aviation from the skies into space. Some wartime inventions, such as the tank, are only suited to war, but many have other uses. The antibiotic penicillin, which saves many lives, was invented in 1941 to cure the infected wounds of soldiers. It is impossible to say whether more good has come from wartime inventions than bad. But one thing is certain, many things were invented *because* of war.

GUIDED MISSILES
All modern strategic missiles and space rockets were developed from the work of a team of Second World War German scientists, who created more than 20 types of missiles. Air-to-air guided missiles, such as this one, are used for aerial combat.

ARMORED TANK
The tank lurched onto First World War battlefields in 1916, thanks to the combined efforts of a number of inventors and British army officers. This modern United Nations tank has a swiveling gun turret and lookout post.

Modern armor
Heavy steel armor plating was first used in America in 1862 to strengthen warships. Today's tanks are encased in lightweight but strong metal alloys, plastics and even ceramics.

RADIO DETECTION AND RANGING
In 1935, the scientist Robert Watson-Watt was asked by the British army to invent a "radio death ray" for warfare. Instead, he invented radar, which detects enemy aircraft using radio waves.

STEALTH FIGHTERS

Difficult to detect because of their shape and a radar absorbent coating, F-117 fighter bombers are designed for precision attack. They were used by the United States in the Gulf War in 1991.

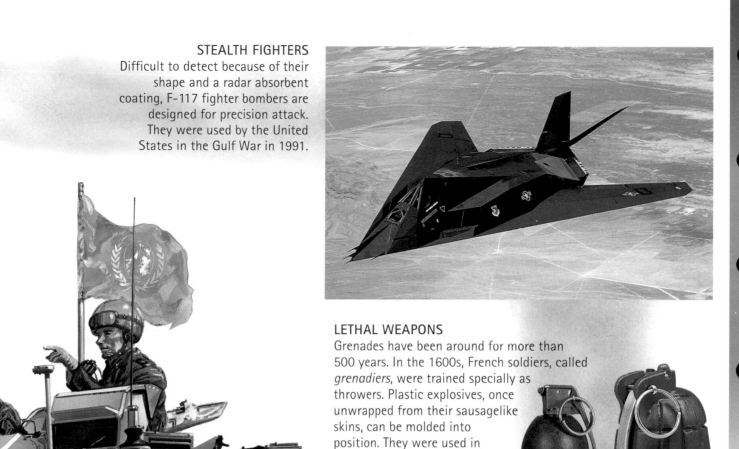

LETHAL WEAPONS

Grenades have been around for more than 500 years. In the 1600s, French soldiers, called *grenadiers*, were trained specially as throwers. Plastic explosives, once unwrapped from their sausagelike skins, can be molded into position. They were used in military operations to shatter parts of bridges and buildings.

PE4
WGT. 8oz (227g)
170 x 35 mm DIA

NIGHT VISION

Since the 1940s, scientists have been working on devices to make it possible to fight in the dark. Night-vision goggles receive and intensify infrared energy, which is given off as heat by animals and objects. The goggles convert the energy into an image so that soldiers can see at night. In theory, 24-hour war is possible, but nothing has yet been invented to fight the need for sleep.

Caterpillar tracks
In 1904, Benjamin Holt built a tractor that laid down its own track under the rear wheels to travel over mud. A continuous track belt under all the wheels of a tank enables it to break through fences and go over deep gullies.

Discover more in Into Battle

53

Healers and Healing

Two hundred years ago, visiting the doctor was a risky business. Operations were performed without proper anesthetic, open wounds often became infected, and many deadly diseases could not be treated. Today, doctors can vaccinate, anesthetize, sterilize and treat with antibiotics. Dramatic discoveries and ingenious inventions led to these life-saving procedures. In 1928, for example, Alexander Fleming discovered a mold that could fight germs. Twelve years later, Howard Florey and Ernst Chain developed this substance and invented the first antibiotic—penicillin. Many of the tools now used by doctors were invented in the 1800s: the stethoscope, which listens to the heartbeat; the endoscope, which allows doctors to peer inside the body; and the sphygmomanometer, which measures blood pressure.

THE POINT OF IT
A syringe is a piston in a tube that can suck up liquids and then squirt them out. The medical syringe attached to a hypodermic (beneath the skin) needle was perfected in 1853 by Scotsman Alexander Wood.

UNDER ANESTHETIC
Only 200 years ago, patients stayed awake during operations. Many had to be tied or held down. In 1846, American dentist William Morton used the chemical ether to anesthetise a patient while a tumor was removed from the man's neck.

TRADITIONAL MEDICINE

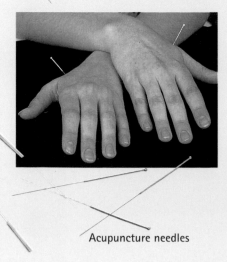

Acupuncture needles

Many cultures treat illnesses with ancient medical inventions. Aboriginal people in Australia make poultices and medicines from bush plants. Tribal shamans in South America combine plants and rituals to make people better. Chinese doctors invented acupuncture more than 2,000 years ago. Acupuncturists insert very fine needles into special points on the body to stimulate the nerves and help the body to heal itself.

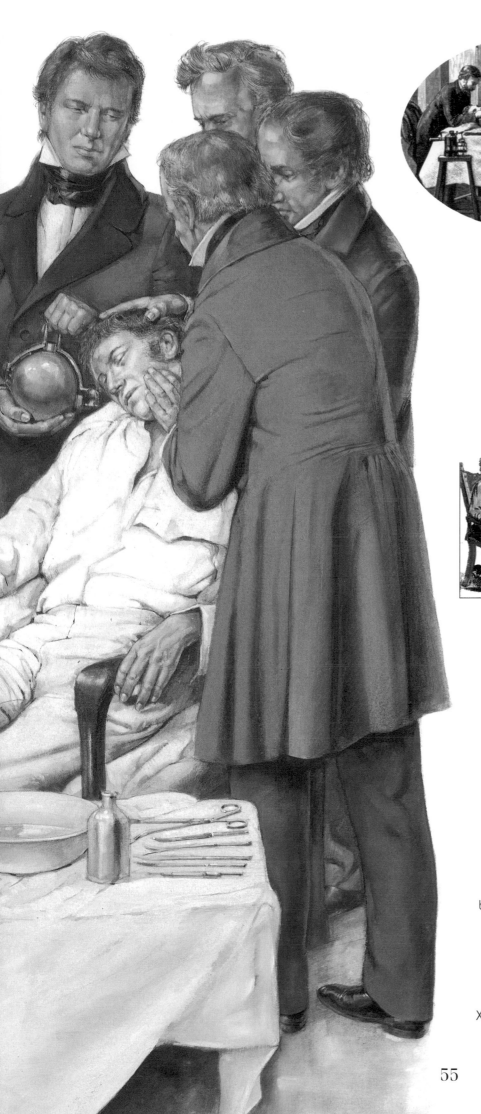

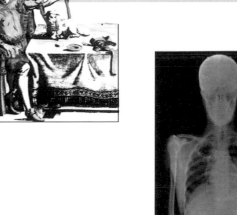

GERM FREE
Doctors once operated with their hands and instruments covered with blood from the previous operation. In 1865, Joseph Lister used carbolic acid to sterilize his hands, tools and the air during an operation.

STRANGE BUT TRUE
In 1667, a blood transfusion was carried out using a lamb as the donor. The patient, a 15-year-old boy who was bleeding to death, survived!

THE BARE BONES
In 1895, German Wilhelm Röntgen discovered a ray that passed through flesh but not through bone. As it was such a mystery ray, he called it X-ray. This marvellous ray was used to take pictures of the human skeleton such as this—the first full-length X-ray of a person, complete with sock suspenders and keys in the pocket.

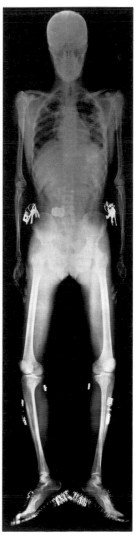

1500 BC
ACUPUNCTURE
China

1270
EYEGLASSES
Court of Kublai Khan
China

1626
MEDICAL THERMOMETER
Santorio
Italy

1796
VACCINATION
Edward Jenner
England

1816
STETHOSCOPE
René Laennec
France

1854
NURSING CORPS
Florence Nightingale
England

1896
SPHYGMOMANO-METER
Scipione Riva-Rocci
Italy

1899
ASPIRIN
Felix Hoffman
Germany

1928
FLYING DOCTOR SERVICE
John Flynn
Australia

AN UNLIKELY PAIR
Embryos of twins can be frozen and then implanted separately, years apart. The result: twins who are not the same age!

Freezing cells
Embryos can be frozen when they consist of only a few cells.

FREEZE–THAW IVF
In 1983, an Australian team led by Carl Wood invented a way to fertilize and grow human embryos in glass tubes and then freeze and store them. The embryos can be thawed and implanted into the womb up to ten years later.

• LIFE AND MEDICINE •

Marvels of Medicine

Medicine has entered an exciting new stage. With today's technology, doctors can now observe the human body working on the inside without cutting it open. Vaccines and genetically engineered viruses can help the body to repair itself, and some inventions can actually replace broken and damaged organs. Artificial parts include electronic ears, plastic stomachs, mechanical hearts, heart pacemakers and ceramic hips. Doctors today use carpentry techniques and stainless steel or plastic nuts, screws and bolts to hold broken bones together. Fifty years ago, these bones never would have healed. Skin, kidneys, heart, liver, ova, sperm, lungs, corneas and bone marrow can be transplanted from person to person. Microsurgery rejoins the smallest blood vessels and nerves that have been cut in accidents.

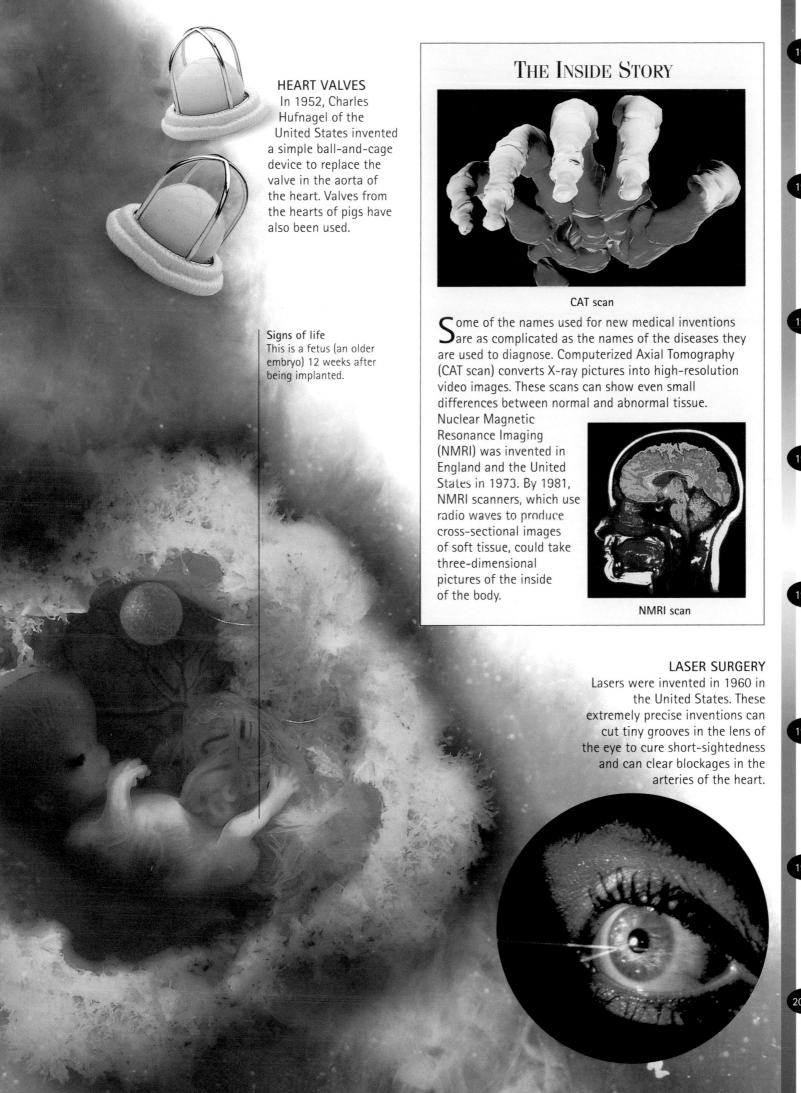

HEART VALVES
In 1952, Charles Hufnagel of the United States invented a simple ball-and-cage device to replace the valve in the aorta of the heart. Valves from the hearts of pigs have also been used.

Signs of life
This is a fetus (an older embryo) 12 weeks after being implanted.

THE INSIDE STORY

CAT scan

Some of the names used for new medical inventions are as complicated as the names of the diseases they are used to diagnose. Computerized Axial Tomography (CAT scan) converts X-ray pictures into high-resolution video images. These scans can show even small differences between normal and abnormal tissue. Nuclear Magnetic Resonance Imaging (NMRI) was invented in England and the United States in 1973. By 1981, NMRI scanners, which use radio waves to produce cross-sectional images of soft tissue, could take three-dimensional pictures of the inside of the body.

NMRI scan

LASER SURGERY
Lasers were invented in 1960 in the United States. These extremely precise inventions can cut tiny grooves in the lens of the eye to cure short-sightedness and can clear blockages in the arteries of the heart.

1900
ELECTRO-CARDIOGRAPH
Willem Einthoven
Netherlands

1927
IRON LUNG RESPIRATOR
Phillip Drinken
USA

1943
ARTIFICIAL KIDNEY MACHINE
Willem Kolff
Netherlands

1954
CONTRACEPTIVE PILL (FEMALE)
G. Pincus and J. Rock
USA

1967
HEART TRANSPLANT
Christiaan Barnard
South Africa

1978
TEST-TUBE BABY
P. Steptoe and R. Edwards
England

1979
BIONIC EAR IMPLANT
G. Clarke
Australia

2000?
SURGICAL ROBOTS

SPOT THE DIFFERENCE
In the future, the spot-making genes from a leopard could be mixed in with the genes of a domestic cat to produce a spotted animal.

KILLER COTTON
In 1992, an American company altered the genes in some cotton plants so that their leaves became poisonous to caterpillars but nothing else. This reduced the need for harmful insecticides.

• LIFE AND MEDICINE •

Biotechnology

We use biotechnology to alter living things. It gives us the power to create new animals, plants, foods, medicines, materials and even machines. People have used biotechnology for thousands of years to slowly breed new plants, animals and the microorganisms that make cheese, bread, beer, yogurt and wine. In 1987, geneticist Truda Straede of Australia created spotted cats after breeding tortoiseshell cats with Burmese and Abyssinian cats for ten years. Today, modern biotechnology could speed up this breeding process by altering the genetic material deep inside living cells. Scientists have already created bright blue carnations, and tomatoes that ripen on the vine without getting mushy. Biotechnology's potential is enormous. We can even use bacteria grown in laboratories to digest oil to clean up oil spills. The next hundred years will be an age of exciting "bio-inventions."

STRANGE BUT TRUE

In 1994, scientists in Australia invented a way of removing fleece from sheep without shearing. They injected sheep with a special hormone then wrapped them in lightweight hairnets. Three weeks later, the fleece could be peeled off the sheep by hand.

TRANSGENIC PIGS

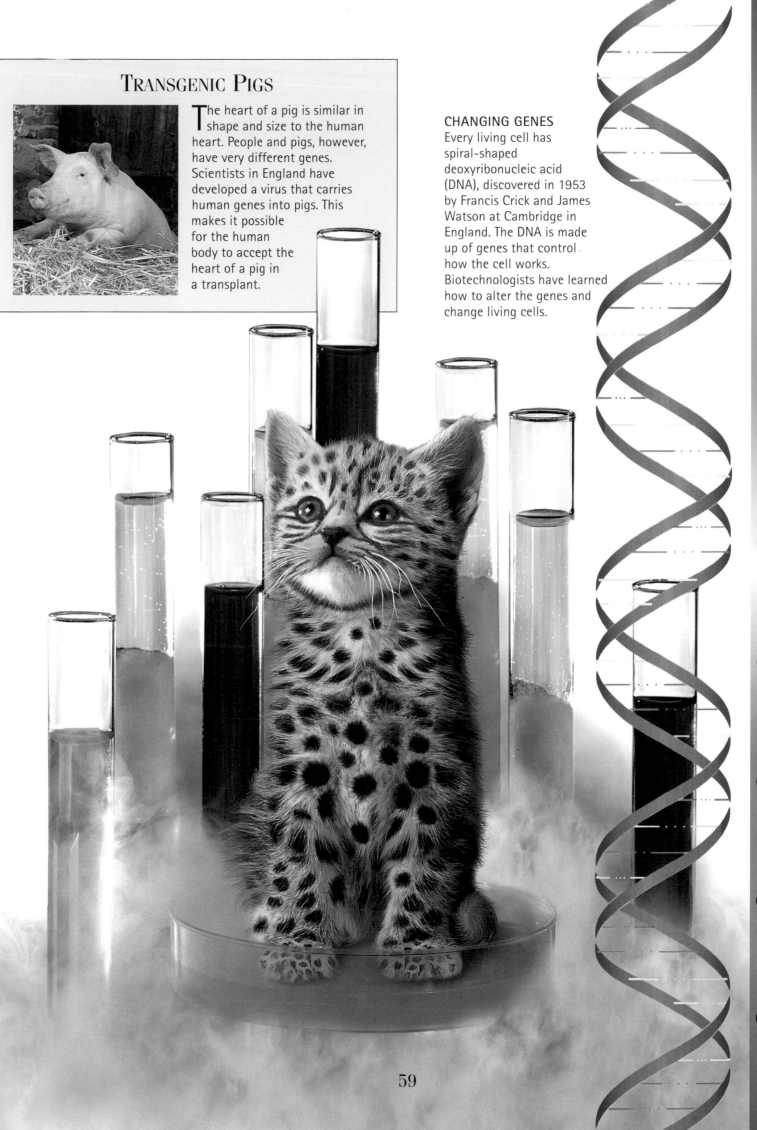

The heart of a pig is similar in shape and size to the human heart. People and pigs, however, have very different genes. Scientists in England have developed a virus that carries human genes into pigs. This makes it possible for the human body to accept the heart of a pig in a transplant.

CHANGING GENES

Every living cell has spiral-shaped deoxyribonucleic acid (DNA), discovered in 1953 by Francis Crick and James Watson at Cambridge in England. The DNA is made up of genes that control how the cell works. Biotechnologists have learned how to alter the genes and change living cells.

6000 BC
BEER
Mesopotamia

1000 BC
CHEESE
Nomad tribes
Middle East

1972
OIL-DIGESTING MICROBES
Dr Ananda M. Chakrabarty
USA

1975
MONOCLONAL ANTIBODY
George Kohler and Cesar Milstein
England

1984
TRANSGENIC PLANT
University of Ghent
Belgium

1986
BLACK TULIP
Geert Hageman
Netherlands

1989
GENE SHEARS
Haseloff and Gerlach
Australia, France, USA

1990
CROWN GALL BACTERICIDE
Dr Alan Kerr
Australia

1991
LONG-LIFE TOMATO
USA

59

It Might Have Been!

The history of invention is full of brilliant, yet crazy ideas. Can you imagine what life might be like today if Thomas Edison had developed his idea of anti-gravity underwear, or if Alexander Bell had persisted in trying to invent a talking fire alarm rather than a telephone? Inventions inspire people to think of the future and its possibilities, but trying to predict the success of inventions and how people will react to them has never been easy. The first motor cars had to travel through towns at walking pace behind a man carrying a red flag because they frightened people and horses. People thought that motor cars would never replace the horse and buggy. In the 1950s, the president of IBM predicted that, at most, no more than one computer per country would ever be built! The computer endured, but other inventions had a short life. This collection from the past 200 years shows you just what might have been.

The umbrella cap
The umbrella, invented thousands of years ago in China, has been the subject of hundreds of improvements. These include a gutter, ventilation holes, folding mechanisms, see-through plastic, and this capbrella from about 1904.

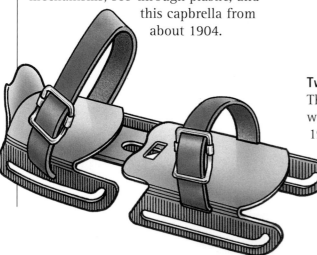

Up and over
In the early 1900s, many railway systems used single tracks. This patent from 1904 shows how an express train could drive over the top of an all-stations train and double the number of passengers on the line. But imagine being a passenger!

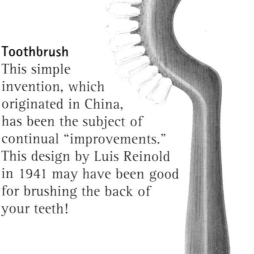

Toothbrush
This simple invention, which originated in China, has been the subject of continual "improvements." This design by Luis Reinold in 1941 may have been good for brushing the back of your teeth!

Two-blade ice skates
These adjustable ice skates were designed by Ralph Hammond in 1934 to fit a wide range of foot sizes. They may have been useful for people who had trouble balancing on one blade, but how would you be able to steer?

Watch out!
In the early days of motor cars, pedestrians and cars were always at odds in the battle for the roadways. The car above was a fanciful invention that vacuumed up "jaywalkers" who strayed onto the road.

Anti-gravity underwear
This 1878 cartoon illustrates the effect of Thomas Edison's anti-gravity underwear. If this ingenious idea had become a reality, wearers would have beaten the Wright brothers in the race to become airborne.

Helicycle

In 1936, Igor Sikorsky's helicopter became the first practical machine to hover in the air. It caught the imagination of Daniel Gumb in 1945, who invented the personal helicopter based on the design of a motorcycle.

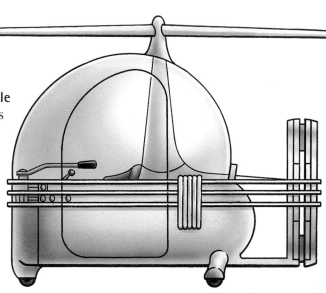

Robot farmers

In the age of steam, some people predicted that farmers would be able to put their feet up; steam-powered robots would do all the heavy farming work. Two hundred years later, tractors and harvesters are fast and efficient, but these machines still need to be operated by farmers.

Folding baby carriage

This is a drawing of a folding carriage patented in the 1890s. The wheels came off and the whole thing folded up into a handbag. A very successful baby carriage that folded up into a neat package was patented by Harold Cornish of Australia in 1942.

Pedestrian scoop

In the 1920s, road fatalities involving pedestrians rose dramatically, as cars became faster while their brakes remained primitive. This led to quite a few inventions that would scoop up pedestrians or bounce them out of the way.

Leg power

This design for a pedal-driven propeller on the back of a surfboard was drawn by Bert Lee in 1942. Today's surfskiers use a paddle to power their crafts through the waves.

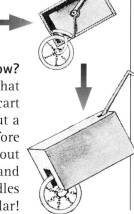

A wheelbarrow?

In 1884, this trunk that becomes a luggage cart was patented—about a hundred years before travel cases with pop-out caster wheels and retracting handles became popular!

Glossary

Quill

Navigational astrolabe

Chopsticks

Box "brownie" camera

Robot

air pressure The force of the air inside a container or in the Earth's atmosphere.

anesthetic A drug that keeps the body from feeling pain and other sensations.

assembly line Part of the mass-production method of manufacturing. Workers fit one part to a product as it moves past them on a conveyor system.

automaton A mechanical figure or toy that moves by itself. It was originally powered and controlled by clockwork.

axial combine harvester A small grain harvester that separates grain in a spinning cage.

bactericide A chemical that kills bacteria.

ballistic missile A missile that is launched into the air by an explosive force then continues to fly by itself. Its flight depends on gravity and its own weight rather than the use of further external force or power.

biotechnology The process of changing or controlling living things to make new products.

board game A game that uses markers on a flat surface or board to indicate progress.

calculator A machine that can add, subtract, multiply and divide numbers.

carbon paper Paper that has been coated with carbon dust. It may be placed between two pieces of plain paper so that anything written on the top piece of paper is copied onto the bottom piece.

CD-ROM An abbreviation for "compact disc read-only memory". This refers to a compact disc used with a computer system.

clockwork The cogs, wheels, gears, springs and shafts used to make mechanical clocks work.

code A system of symbols where each symbol represents a different piece of information.

computer A machine that automatically performs calculations according to a set of instructions that are stored in its memory.

contraceptive A chemical or device designed to prevent women from becoming pregnant.

dandy horse A two-wheeled "bike" pushed along with the feet. It was made popular in the early 1800s by fashionable men called "dandies."

dugout canoe A small boat made by hollowing out a log.

electrocardiograph A machine that records the electrical activity of the heart.

electronic circuit The pathways and connections followed by electrons to control computers, robots and modern domestic appliances.

electronic television The modern television system that uses an electron gun to scan images and reproduce them on a cathode-ray tube.

embryo An animal, such as a mammal, in the early stages of its development inside the uterus.

environmentally friendly Machines, appliances and materials that do not damage the natural resources and features of the Earth.

fetus The embryo of an animal in the later stages of its development when it shows the main characteristics of the mature animal.

fossil fuels The remains of animals and plants left in the earth that form coal, oil and natural gas over millions of years.

graphite A soft, grey-black form of carbon used in pencils.

gravity The force of attraction towards the Earth that keeps everything on the ground.

guided missile An airborne bomb that can chase a moving target. It may be guided by wires, radio controls, laser light or infrared sensors.

gunpowder A mixture of potassium nitrate, sulphur and charcoal used as an explosive and in fireworks.

hydroponics The growing of plants by placing their roots in water enriched with nutrients rather than in soil.

Inuit A dweller of the Arctic region who is sometimes called an Eskimo.

invention An original or new product or process.

irrigation The system of supplying the land with an artificial water supply using pumps, pipes and channels.

IVF An abbreviation for "in vitro fertilization," which refers to the artificial fertilization of an egg in order to produce embryos.

laser A very intense light of one wavelength and frequency that can travel long distances. It is used to cut materials (including flesh), carry television transmissions, print onto paper and guide machines.

locomotive A self-powered vehicle that runs on a railway track.

mass production A method of manufacturing large quantities of goods, often using a number of machines. Each worker or machine in a factory works on just one part of a product.

memory The part of a computer that stores data and instructions.

microsurgery Surgery conducted using specially designed microscopes and tiny instruments to repair the smallest parts of the body.

monoclonal antibody An antibody produced in the laboratory that can be used to detect diseases and immunize people and animals against them.

optical fiber A communications cable made of solid glass or plastic fiber. It transmits light from one end to the other, even when the cable is curved or bent.

ornithopter A flying machine that propels itself through the air by means of flapping wings.

papyrus A kind of paper made from the papyrus plant. It was used by the ancient Egyptians, Greeks and Romans.

patent A law that guarantees inventors the exclusive rights to perfect, build, sell and operate their inventions for a number of years.

percussion instrument A musical instrument that produces sound when it is struck by the hand or a hammer.

piston A movable, solid cylinder that is forced to go up and down inside a tube by the exertion of pressure.

pitch How high or low a musical note is when compared to other musical notes.

poultice A medical pack or dressing placed on part of the body to cure a sickness or soothe an inflammation.

program Instructions given to and stored in the memory of a computer so that it can carry out a particular task.

radar Stands for "radio detecting and ranging." This is a way of locating an object by measuring the time and direction of a returning radio wave.

radio waves Invisible electromagnetic waves that carry information such as Morse code "beeps" and the human voice.

Renaissance The period in Europe between 1300 and 1500 when science, invention, art and education were strongly encouraged.

rivet A metal pin or bolt used for holding two or more pieces of a material together.

shaman A medicine man or woman with special powers to heal and contact the spirits.

shorthand writing A fast type of handwriting where simple strokes represent parts of words.

sonar Stands for "sound navigation and ranging." A device that sends sound through water and then detects echoes as they bounce off the sea floor and other objects.

sterilize To kill germs on instruments and in the air.

synthesizer A machine that electronically creates and amplifies musical sounds.

technology The tools and methods for applying scientific knowledge to everyday life.

totalizator A machine for calculating, recording and indicating a system of betting on horse races.

transgenic Containing genetic features that have been artificially transferred from a different species.

turbine A wheel with many blades that is made to turn by a gas such as steam, or a liquid such as water. It is used to power machines or to generate electricity.

type A piece of rectangular metal with a raised letter or symbol on one side.

velocipede An early form of bicycle that looked like the dandy horse.

virtual reality An artificial environment produced by a computer that seems very real to the person experiencing it.

virus A microorganism that can only reproduce inside a living cell.

Padlock

Dandy horse

Electric iron

String telephone

Pitchfork

63

Index

Picture Credits

(t=top, b=bottom, l=left, r=right, c=center, i=icon, F=front, C=cover, B=back, Bg=background)
Ad-Libitum, 4tl, 4bl, 4it, 4ic, 4ib, 4tr, 5itc, 5ic, 5ibc, 5ib, 5tl, 6/7c, 6/7/8/9, 8i, 9tr, 10i, 12c, 12i, 13i, 14i, 14tl, 14tr, 15tc, 15tl, 16/17c, 16i, 16tl, 18i, 18c, 18tl, 20i, 21br, 22i, 23i, 24i, 26i, 27i, 30i, 32i, 34l, 35c, 36bl, 38tc, 38l, 39br, 39cr, 39tl, 40/41c, 40lc, 42i, 43br, 43tr, 44l, 44i, 46i, 48i, 50i, 51c, 52i, 54 bl, 54i, 56i, 58i, 59c, 62cl, 63br, 63tr, 62bcl (S. Bowey), 25cr, (S. Bowey/Australian National Maritime Museum), 46cl, 63cr (S. Bowey/Kellett's Museum of Laundry Irons, Melbourne), 44cr (N. Vinnicombe). **Air Portraits**, 5tr, 26cl (D. Davies). **AKG**, 39bl, (E. Bohr), 9tl (Wurttembergisches Landesmuseum, Stuttgart). **Ancient Art and Architecture Collection**, 41cr. **Art Resource**, 27tl, 28tl (Scala). **Australian Museum**, 50l (C. Bento). **Australian Picture Library**, 37bl, 63bcr (M. Adams), 12bl (Archive Photos), 11cr, 17tr (Bettmann Archive), 7br (E.T. Archives), 48/49c (D. & J. Heaton), 25tr, 46tl, **Austral International**, 56tl (Rex Features London/*The Sun*). **Aviation Picture Library**, 53cr (J. Flack). **Black Star**, 43cr (M. Balderas), 41c. **Bridgeman Art Library**, 40bl (British Museum, London), 41br (British Library). **Brilliant Images**, 19br. **British Film Institute**, 38tr, 38/39c (BFI Stills). **Brownel & Wight Car Company 1890**, 21tr. **Caroma Industries**, 11br. **Check Six**, 53tr (J. Benson). **Bruce Coleman Ltd**, 15cr (D. & M. Plage), 48tc (J. Cancalosi), 58tl (J. Foott), 58bl, 59tl (H. Reinhard). **Coo-ee Picture Library**, 38bl (R. Ryan). **Crown Equipment**, 12tr. **Culver Pictures**, 7tr. **Department of Defence**, 53br, 53cl. **Deutsches Museum Munich**, 55br. **Edison National Historic Site USA**, 47tr. **E.T. Archives**, 1c, 36c (Science Museum). **Mary Evans Picture Library**, 23tr,

51tr, 51br, 60br, 60cr, 61cr, 61tl. **Granger Collection**, 27br, 28br, 29tl, 30bc, 30br. **Robert Harding Picture Library**, 13tl (R. Evans), 29tr, 39tr, 42l, 49t. **Hoover Co**, Nth Canton Ohio, 11tr. **Illustrated London News Picture Library**, 60cl, 60 tr, 61br, 61c. **Image Bank**, 5i, 17i, 34i, 36i, 38i, 40i (L. Reupert), 49cr (L.J. Pierce). **Image Select**, 32i, 34i (Ann Ronan Picture Library). **International Photo Library**, 52tr. **Loren McIntyre**, 42tr. **Mansell Collection Ltd**, 35tl. **Mattel Toys**, 18bl. **Military Picture Library**, 52bl, 53cr. **Jenny Mills**, 24tr. **Lego Australia**, 19tr. **NASA**, 32br, 32cr. **National Museum of Roller Skating, Lincoln, Nebraska**, 19tl. **Lennart Nilsson**, 56/57c. **Nobel Foundation**, 4i, 6i, 6l, 6r. **Peraves Ltd**, 23cr. **Peter Newark's American Pictures**, 31br. **Photo Researchers Inc**, 12tl (A. Green), 40br (S. McCartney), 20tr, 21cr. **Polperro Pictures**, 22tr (B. Geach). **Powerhouse Museum**, Sydney, 34tr, 36tl, 41tr, 46bl. **Royal Aeronautical Society**, 26tl. **Royal North Shore Hospital**, Sydney, 57tl. **Science Museum**, 45br (D. Exton), 30ct, 54tl, (Science & Society Picture Library), 24tl, 43tl, 43bl, 47br, 62tcl. **Smithsonian Institution**, 32tl, 48tl. **Spectrum Colour Library**, 15br, 25bl. **Stock Photos Pty Ltd**, 14/15c (P. Steel), 24bl (D. Madison). **The Photo Library**, 57tr (R. Chase), 58tr (P. Hayson), 48/49c (N. Hong), 50tr (Hulton-Deutsch), 49r (W. Kent), 44bl (W. & C. McIntyre), 57br (Photo Researchers Inc /S. Camazine), 32cl (Science Photo Library), 59r (Science Photo Library), 48/49c (R. Smith), 5br, 49br (Science Photo Library/B. Blokhuis), 54cl (Science Photo Library/O. Burriel), 48tr (Science Photo Library/J. Mead), 57br (Science Photo Library/A. Tsiaras), 9cr W. Stacey), 44tr, 62bl (U.S. Dept of Energy), 59c (Tony Stone Worldwide), 39bc, 56/57c, 56cl. **Topham**, 31cr. **Victa**, 10bl. **Werner Forman Archive**,

34lc (British Museum, London). **Wheels Magazine**, 48/49c (W. Kent). **Xerox Corporation**, 17br, 17cr. **Yamaha Japan**, 41tl.

Photo Manipulation

Richard Wilson Studios, 6/7, 8/9, 48/49, 56/57, 58/59.

Illustration Credits

Graham Back, 34tc, 35r, 44cr, 62tl, David Boehm, 44l, Gregory Bridges, 2/3, 27/28/29/30c, 28bl, 30r, 44/45c. Leslye Cole, 46/47c. Christer Eriksson, 18/19c. Mike Golding, 26/31c, 31tr. Christa Hook/Bernard Thornton Artists, UK, 36/37c. Richard Hook/Bernard Thornton Artists, UK, 54/55c. Gillian Jenkins, 22tl, 22br, 22cr, 22cl, 63tcr. Mike Lamble, 10/11c. Connell Lee, 32/33c. Iain McKellar, 42c. David Nelson, 38/39c. Stephen Seymour/Bernard Thornton Artists, UK, 52/53c. Ray Sim, 47cr, Mark Sofilas, 15tr. 50/51c. Kevin Stead, 24/25c. Ross Watton/Garden Studio, 12/13c, 21tl, 20/21c. Rod Westblade, 22/23, 50bl, 60bl, 60c, 61bl, 61tr, endpapers.

Cover Credits

Ad-Libitum, FCcr, FCtr, FCtl, (S. Bowey). Gregory Bridges, BCbr. Esselte Letraset Limited, FCbg. Richard Wilson Studios, FCc. The Photo Library, BCtl (U.S. Dept of Energy). Wheels Magazine, FCc (W. Kent).